Joe

expert gardening guide

create your own
nature
garden

Collins

Published by Collins
An imprint of HarperCollins Publishers
Westerhill Road, Bishopbriggs, Glasgow G64 2QT
www.harpercollins.co.uk
collins.reference@harpercollins.co.uk

HarperCollins Publishers
1st Floor, Watermarque Building, Ringsend Road,
Dublin 4, Ireland

A catalogue record for this book is available from
the British Library

ISBN 978-0-00-846110-2

10 9 8 7 6 5 4 3 2 1

Printed in Slovenia by GPS Group

Thanks to my agents, Charlotte Robertson and
Debbie Scheisse, and everyone at HarperCollins
Publishers including Gerry Breslin, Gordon
MacGilp, Lauren Murray and Kevin Robbins.

Photo credits
page 11 © RM Floral / Alamy Stock Photo;
page 12 © Photos Horticultural / Alamy Stock
Photo; page 14 © Ed Brown / Alamy Stock
Photo; page 15 © Jacky Parker Photography
/ Getty Images; page 16 © Beata Aldridge /
Alamy Stock Photo; page 19 © Annette Lepple
/ Alamy Stock Photo; page 21 © Alex Ramsay
/ Alamy Stock Photo; page 25 © Tim Gainey /
Alamy Stock Photo; page 163 © Frank Hecker
/ Alamy Stock Photo; page 182 © Elizabeth
Ann Duffy / EyeEm / Getty Images; page 186
© brytta / Getty Images; page 187 © Claudia
Wizner / Alamy Stock Photo; page 198 ©
Photimageon / Alamy Stock Photo; page 210 ©
mrod / Getty Images; page 211 © keith burdett
/ Alamy Stock Photo

All other images © Shutterstock.com

Joe's

expert gardening guide

create your own

nature
garden

introduction

garden layout   9
general gardening approach   17
wildlife corridors   23
wildlife ponds   27
birds   35
bugs, beetles and other insects   83
hedgehogs   93
amphibians   99
bats   109
bees and other pollinators   117

butterflies and moths   135
going organic   149
organic pest control   157
wildflower meadows   163
collecting seed from your own garden   173
native hedges   179
rain gardens   187
annuals   195
planting a tree   209

index   217

introduction

To be surrounded by and spending time observing nature is one of life's great pleasures. I take plenty of inspiration for gardening and designing outdoor spaces from the natural world, perhaps observing the way a group of plants interacts and colonises a landscape or noting the way water playfully cascades through a brook. A garden, of course, is not a wild landscape. It's a managed, often stylised, space – a hybrid of our desires and nature's way – yet, to me, a garden will only feel 'truly alive' if it's buzzing with bees, fluttering with butterflies and with plenty of birdsong as a backing track.

Sadly, the decline of wildlife (in the UK) over the years has been well documented, the result of a host of reasons (modern and monocultural farming methods, population growth, loss of habitat, etc.). It can make for depressing reading, yet we can help to slow the decline and hopefully reverse areas of it too by making sure that any outside space we have access to is overseen with wildlife in mind.

Gardens are not just a small part of the equation. There are an estimated 16 million gardens in the UK which, when combined, cover an area larger than all of our nature reserves put together. You could say our largest nature reserve is one big garden! The range of plants and habitats within them is exceptionally rich and varied too; a vital resource for the wildlife they support.

We can really make a difference in the way we manage the soil and the choice and range of plants we grow throughout the year, from tall trees down to tiny spring-flowering bulbs. Considering each decision along the way for its environmental benefits only adds depth to the narrative of our plots, making them richer and more interesting.

It's also a misconception that 'wildlife-friendly gardens' have to be unkempt, perhaps rather messy plots. 'Design' is simply the act of planning and bringing the elements together for both their form and their function. If one of the functions is to increase biodiversity within a garden, it doesn't mean it can't look great too. It's a two-way street as well, because the more biodiverse a garden is, the healthier it tends to be: a rich ecosystem invites predators, so is less prone to pest infestations and diseases.

There are many projects that we can all do: bug hotels, bird feeders, planting for pollinators or making a hedgehog house. Kids are the future custodians of our planet and love to get involved and what a fine way of encouraging them to engage with nature. It doesn't take much effort (often the opposite – do less!) or necessarily cost anything at all.

The way I garden, I certainly feel like I'm managing the space sensitively and doing my bit for wildlife. Yet, gardening this way I don't feel as if I'm in a bubble; I feel I'm part of something far bigger than the space within my garden boundaries. Get on board, see your plot as an exciting Nature Garden, an important resource, and together we really can make a difference.

garden layout

As a garden designer, I always like spaces to flow nicely, look great, have direction and ultimately function well. A nature garden is simply any garden that puts an emphasis on the function of encouraging and sustaining wildlife. Throw away your preconceptions of what a 'wildlife garden' is. As long as it has a high proportion of vegetation, it can be a very stylish space too, the wildlife doesn't care! A nature garden can be made from scratch; an existing garden will probably require some adaptations or have some key elements added into it to make it more welcoming and biodiverse. The three requirements that we all need in life are food, water and shelter and it's exactly the same for all animals. Walk around your garden and consider how you can make every single element of it more attractive to wildlife. Perhaps you've inherited a garden, are looking to tweak areas over time, or starting one from scratch? Here are some pointers to consider.

So who needs a lawn, eh?

Surfaces and paths

Large areas of unbroken barren paving don't support any life and don't allow access for burrowing animals. If constructing any new surfaces, look for those that are free draining (gravels/aggregates/slate chippings/woodchip/paviours with gaps incorporated and the paviours laid on sand without cement). Look to incorporate and introduce spaces and gaps for planting wherever possible, which will soften it visually too. With existing paving, is there any way you can lift slabs or units, dig out the subbase and put soil in for more planting? Water runoff from hard paved areas can lead to drainage issues and puddling, yet ideally it seeps directly back into the water table rather than just going down the drain (see the rain gardens chapter). The siting and size of paths are worth thinking about too. Rather than butting directly up to a fence or boundary wall, leave a generous border as a wildlife corridor. A narrow path for a single person will be much narrower than a path for two to walk side-by-side, yet in a small garden it is probably enough and will provide more space for vegetation.

hedges

We love hedges! They flower, often berry, provide extremely important cover, filter winds and reduce pollution in towns and cities. They can be grown as a boundary instead of (or as well as) a fence or wall (see the native hedges chapter) yet are significantly better for wildlife. They can also look great as part of the planting structure within a garden space to help organise it into 'rooms' or create privacy where required.

climbers

Walls and fences are similar to hard surfaces but on the vertical. Old walls may have some cracks/nooks/crannies for insects to nest in (and look to include these if making from scratch) but in truth most are pretty unfriendly. Greening these up with climbing plants and wall shrubs (honeysuckle/ivy/pyracantha/wisteria/clematis/ climbing roses, etc.) counteracts these harsh elements and provides cover and food for a host of animals. It will make the garden feel softer and often larger too as you visually lose the edges of the space.

A fabulous virginia creeper in autumn and a wildlife sanctuary in spring and summer ...

water

Water in some form or other is an essential element in a nature garden. Plan it into the garden layout on the ground using a spray can, string or hosepipe to get an idea of position and size. Be as generous as you can be with its size and shape as it will visually shrink when full. Avoid siting it under deciduous trees and shrubs (to avoid leaves dropping in and fouling the water) but I find a little shade helps keep the water cool and stops it turning green in spring. Ideally, a pond is surrounded by soft landscaping most of the way round, with plants to provide shelter and access for the host of animals that will use it (see the wildlife ponds chapter).

seating

Seating areas may not be part of a garden's remit for wildlife but if you count yourself as one of the garden visitors too, you'll need somewhere to sit, observe and enjoy! It's an important part of a garden layout (how big, how many people to sit, some garden owners love to sit in sun, others in shade, etc.). Think about how you can bring bee and butterfly-friendly plants as close as possible to where you're sitting (borders cutting into a seating area or large containers) as well as opening up and framing a longer view or two across the wider garden. Additional benches and seats can always be placed precisely where you want them (perhaps next to a pond or in the shade of a tree?) as a perfect vantage point, which in turn gives the garden a destination point or two. Their placing may have a knock-on effect on the design layout as you may need an extra path or a few stepping stones to get to them.

wildlife corridors

When considering your layout, see the elements as working together and joining together too so that, if at all possible, wildlife can move freely under cover without meeting obstacles. Gaps in boundary walls and fences encourage the movement of hedgehogs between gardens but within a garden plot, try to connect up all the green spaces too. Small, isolated borders within paved areas are best avoided as are thin borders where it's hard to get a decent volume of vegetation. A long path without breaks in it all the way down one side of a space can form a barrier to movement. Imagine you're a mini beast and want the freedom to get all around the garden without obstruction by only walking on soil or perhaps gravel. Try to define any obvious jams and you can hone in on areas where things can be improved such as lifting slabs, losing some lawn or perhaps sloping areas of the garden rather than putting in retaining walls.

Log stacks and dead wood habitats

As part of a nature-friendly garden, a pile of logs can be thrown anywhere in the garden, right? Yes, that is pretty much correct, but get creative and they can also double up as part of the integral structure and exciting design of the garden too. They can be sculptural and/or functional, made into divisions, boundaries, seating, etc., as well as making fine visual foils for any planting in front.

general
gardening
approach

Before getting into the detail of how to encourage certain species into your garden with habitats and plants, it's well worth looking at what's already in it and taking an overview on where you're generally heading with it. This may have a bearing on what you dig up or choose to leave in too. You may have gardened in a particular way for years, and perhaps now's the time to tweak those habits with nature in mind.

Layering planting heights

The space above ground level in your garden is yours all the way up to the moon (and beyond), yet so many people mostly garden below knee level! Look at your space three-dimensionally and in layers with an aim to get more volume of plants in it overall; as a rule, the more plants the better. From top to bottom we can layer the planting with trees (appropriate ones for small gardens of course), shrubs, climbers, perennials, grasses, herbs, bulbs, edibles ... right down to ground cover to fill in gaps that would otherwise be bare soil on show. We now have far more scope to cover more bases, tick more wildlife boxes and I guarantee your garden will look better for longer throughout the seasons as a result too.

Have a diverse range of plants

The ideal garden has areas of sun and shade to grow a wide range of plants. Dappled shade can easily be introduced by planting a tree or large shrub that also provides cover and, if chosen well, will flower and berry too. Nature gardens certainly don't have to be made up of solely native plants, which would be difficult to achieve and pretty underwhelming to look at year-round. A

diverse range of plants from all over the world creates a particularly rich environment for wildlife to thrive.

choose plants for wildlife

As you go through this book, there'll be many plants mentioned and the specific reasons given for why they're good for nature (good for pollinators, berries for birds, climbers for nesting, etc.). Use them as a base for your garden palette. When you buy a plant, consider its qualities, and how it helps. For example, you may have your eye on a couple of perennials. One has simple, honest, open single flowers (easy for bees, etc. to access). The other is a hybrid double with closed petals and little scent, which may look pretty (if a little blousy), but is far less beneficial to pollinators. Which one would you choose? Thought so, me too!

Long season of interest

Your garden may look great and be rich in key plants at certain times of the year, but gardening with nature in mind we're looking to even out the highs and lows to extend the food resource for as long as possible. It's pretty easy to fill your garden with nectar-rich plants in spring and summer but consider early (like viburnums, sarcococca and daphnes) and late-flowering plants (sedum and many daisies) as well as spring bulbs and some berrying plants to help during the more barren months.

pruning

We prune for many different reasons such as keeping a plant to a certain size, increasing flowering or improved stem colour, letting light and air into its crown (so reducing fungal diseases) and to filter light beneath (to benefit lower-storey plants). Sometimes it's for plant hygiene reasons (pruning off some dead or rubbing branches to stop them dying back into the main stem) and of course the aesthetics too, to balance a plant and make it stand proud. In the wild, plants aren't pruned, they may get nibbled, munched, used as a scratching post, broken in a storm, etc., and dead wood eventually falls on the ground and decays. In our garden, plants are part of the manipulated garden setting. How much or little you prune is up to you and you'll find a balance that works for you and your garden. Deadheading some plants (such as annuals and repeat-flowering roses) encourages them to flower for longer, which is likely to be beneficial, but on the flip side, those roses may not produce hips for the birds. Experiment one year to the next and see what works. Another scenario is that you may have some beneficial trees, shrubs or hedges that are overgrown and out of hand. You may be thinking about taking them out altogether, but with some considered pruning (lifting the crown, thinning, cutting hard back to regenerate) they could be turned into a huge asset for you and nature.

cutting back grasses and perennials

When I first started gardening, we'd obsessively cut back perennials and grasses the minute they looked as if they were 'going over', which was all part of the school ethos of 'immaculate, yet wildlife-unfriendly gardens'. Followers of the new perennial movement (pioneered by the likes of Piet Oudolf and James van Sweden) planted huge swathes of perennials and grasses together instead of lawns, demonstrating just how beautiful these plants are in decay and how many hold their dried form through the winter months and look great when frosted. This approach is the way to go, being so much better for wildlife in general as the plants provide cover and nesting sites. Some plants (like the dried flower spike of a tall Verbascum) are complete multi-storey bug hotels in themselves. These days, I tend to let plants keel over, leaving them till the last minute in late winter before cutting back and composting.

Lawn

Ah, the great British lawn, stripes and all! Okay, so we are obsessed with mown grass in our gardens, which isn't great when looking to encourage wildlife. Lawns are monocultural, so support minimal wildlife. The smaller a garden is, the less practical a lawn is, receiving more wear per square metre (which leads to compaction). They are often a mud bath in winter and need regular mowing (often with polluting mowers) and other care (watering, scarifying, feeding, aerating), which usually makes lawns the highest maintenance part of any garden. I'm always advising people to 'lose the small lawn' and perhaps put a few stepping stones or gravel in, perhaps packing it with a range of plants, including some low growers, to tiptoe through. In larger gardens, I appreciate that a lawn is an economic surface to put down and perhaps more practical to maintain but do consider reducing the areas you mow, let at least some of the grass grow long and look to introduce some wildflowers (see the wildflower meadows chapter). With the more manicured areas, if you reduce the regularity and height you cut it, clover and trefoils will grow and flower for bees. Yes, they may be seen as lawn weeds (oh no!) by some, but are part and parcel of the nature lover's armoury.

wildlife corridors

Wildlife, or biological, corridors are important as they link habitats together so that the population of a species doesn't become isolated and dependant on the resources and habitats of one area. In the wider landscape, they tend to be linear features in the form of ditches and streams, hedgerows, field margins, avenues of trees and motorway verges. Man-made tunnels and underpasses also allow wildlife to move freely from one side of a road to another. If a linear feature is broken with gaps, it loses some of its function but can still be an important 'stepping stone' for dispersal and migration.

Now, you may have turned your garden into a successful wildlife haven with loads of different species turning up at will – a success! All manner of wildlife will both come and go if it can, which is not a problem for those with wings or those that can easily climb fences, but for others it's not so easy.

Hedgehogs are a good example. They love to move around. You may spot one so regularly that you think it

lives in your garden but it's quite likely to just be visiting as they move around a lot in search of food, often up to 2 miles a night! They hate to be boxed in, so consider how a hedgehog might get in and out of your garden and into your neighbour's and beyond without having to go out onto a dangerous road. A simple hole in the fence (around 15–20 cm all around) at ground level will do the job nicely and allow other animals through too. Yes, you can make small holes in existing brick and block walls too but get an expert in to make sure it's safe and support the rest of the wall with a small lintel. If you're installing new boundaries, include hedgehog access from the get-go.

If you can team up with your neighbours and connect your gardens together in simple ways (holes in boundaries, good tree cover between them, I've even seen a water feature going from one neighbour's garden through a hole in the wall to the next-door garden), it can be hugely beneficial to wildlife. All your gardens put together with the plants and habitats they hold can make the area more biodiverse and greater than the sum of its parts.

wildlife ponds

Water in some form or other is an essential and magical element in a nature garden. Frogs, newts, damselflies, water beetles, pondskaters, birds and more will turn up of their own accord. Small ponds make a great day or weekend project and one to get the kids involved in. As well as being plenty of fun, it will help them to connect with the nature in their own back yard. Of course water, however small or shallow, is always a safety factor with young children, so before launching into it, think about how you can make it 100% safe. Full covers really defeat the object, although metal grid covers can work well. Perhaps you could site it in a corner of the garden that can easily be fenced off with a picket-style fence so that animals can still get through? Although the bigger the better, small is fine – they really don't have to be particularly ambitious. You may have a view on the aesthetics so feel free to make it as fancy as you want, but frankly, wildlife couldn't care what it looks like.

Siting

Make sure the pond will have plenty of planting around it to act as a wildlife corridor rather than sitting in a paved area or lawn. The pond should sit at ground level rather than being raised above ground (which makes it almost impossible for insects, amphibians etc. to get in and out). Ponds like a little shade to reduce the amount of sunlight on the water surface, which can lead to algae problems. On the flipside, ponds don't like to be under deciduous trees as the leaves that fall into them in the autumn will decay, reducing the pond's quality, and ultimately make it smelly and uninhabitable for any creatures. Small ponds can easily be netted over in autumn and pond plants and peripheral plants can be added to shade the water (see below).

Depth

The ideal depth for a wildlife pond is at least 45 cm deep; remember, this is not a fish pond, which has different criteria. You can, however, make wildlife ponds and puddles way shallower if you wish and although it will limit what turns up, some water is better than none.

Lining and edges

Think what you're going to make your pond from and what shape it will be. You can buy pond liners of varying cost and quality in rolls to drop into a pre-dug shape or buy prefabricated shapes in fibreglass with built-in shelves for planting. Admittedly, this can all get a bit fancy so how about recycling an old cold-water storage tank, an old beer barrel or even a deep washing-up bowl or two for a quick fix? They can be made from absolutely anything that can be dropped into a hole in the ground that will hold water. A shallow beach on at least one side is better than steep sides for access. If you have a tank or pond with vertical sides, then build up a ramp inside by placing some stones or small boulders to come up and over the edge. All the edges can be covered by placing some large loose stones on the top. Think nooks and crannies wherever possible to create hideaways for your new guests.

Hornwort is a floating aquatic plant that provides cover for small frogs and other animals.

planting

Plant a mixture of oxygenating, floating and marginal plants to get a good variety of wildlife and to keep your pond water clean and in balance. Native pond plants include marsh marigold, yellow flag, hornwort, water violet and frogbit. Look to cover around 50% of the water's surface with plants to shade the water and help create cover.

marsh marigold

yellow flag

frogbit

water violet

A few dos and don'ts

Do:

- Be patient. The water will always green up in spring but, if well planted, will clear later in the year. It can take a good year for water and plants to reach a proper balance.

- Try to use rainwater to fill it. If you use tap water, leave it a week so that the chlorine can evaporate before planting. Top it up in summer if the level drops.

- Try to get a bucket of good pond water from a friend to add as it will be full of micro-organisms to help speed up the pond's development.

- Keep an eye on blanket weed and clear it by hand. Leave it on the side of the pond for a while so any wildlife can find its way back in.

- Leave rough patches around the edge as a wildlife sanctuary.

Don't:

- Use chemicals in the pond ever. It may upset the balance and will harm wildlife.

- Introduce wildlife yourself. They should come naturally and if they don't, make sure any frogspawn or frogs you do introduce come from a healthy source as they can carry disease.

- Introduce fish, especially goldfish as they'll eat a lot of the native invertebrates and tadpoles. If you want fish, put them in a separate pond.

birds

I love idling the time away watching birds feeding or having a wash in the garden when I should probably be doing something more productive! Many birds live close to and happily alongside the human species, animating our gardens and filling them with song. Birds are drawn to the gardens in which they feel safe and have a plentiful supply of food, with somewhere to perch and perhaps nest in the form of trees, shrubs, climbers and/ or bird boxes. You may not be able to provide them with the complete five-star food and accommodation package in a tiny space, but just a little food and water is usually located by them and most are quick to tell their friends. Since 1979, the RSPB (Royal Society for the Protection of Birds) has invited the British public to get involved in the 'Big Garden Birdwatch'. One spends an hour tracking the birds that come and go in the garden and then submits the results online. It's been hugely successful and a way of monitoring numbers, movement and how they're faring over the years. Birds such as the house sparrow, song thrush and starling have drastically declined since the late 1980s, while collared doves, wood pigeons and coal tit numbers have increased.

Blackbird

One of the most common and easily recognisable birds. The male is black with a bright orange-yellow beak; females are brown with spots and streaks on their breast. Their mellow song is a favourite.

 Size: 25 cm.

 When to spot: All year round.

 Diet: Unfussy. Their diet is varied: insects and worms. Berries and windfall fruit in season.

 On the table: Mealworms, uncooked oats, and dog food.

 Breeding and nesting: Grass/mud nests made in shrubs, hedges and climbers, often low down.

Blue tit

Fabulous colours, a mixture of blue, green and white with a yellow undercarriage. In winter they team up in groups and search for food and look out for each other. A group of a few in the garden is likely to be feeding many more behind the scenes.

 Size: 12 cm.

 When to spot: All year round.

 Diet: Seeds, nuts, caterpillars and insects. Berries in autumn.

 On the table: Peanuts, sunflower seeds and hearts, suet fat.

 Breeding and nesting: Holes in trees and bird boxes and sometimes pipes and holes in brickwork etc.

coal tit

Smaller and not as bright and colourful as other tits being mainly monochrome with shades of whites, greys and blacks. More shy than other tits but common visitors to our gardens. Has a smaller, slender beak adapted for feeding from conifers. Joins groups in winter to feed.

 Size: 12 cm.

 When to spot: All year round.

 Diet: Insects, seeds and nuts.

 On the table: Peanuts, sunflower seeds and hearts, suet fat.

 Breeding and nesting: Holes in trees and bird boxes and sometimes low down like old mouse holes.

Great tit

The largest of our tit species. Has a distinct black head and white cheeks. Very vocal too with a two-note song. It's a woodland bird, highly adapted to our gardens and sometimes likes to show smaller birds who's the boss at the bird table. Teams up with blue tits in winter to search for food.

 Size: 15 cm.

 When to spot: All year round.

 Diet: Insects, seeds, and nuts.

 On the table: Peanuts, sunflower seeds and hearts, suet fat.

 Breeding and nesting: Holes in trees and nest boxes etc.

Goldfinch

Feathered beauty with distinctive bright yellow markings on wings and red face. Lovely squeaky twittering song. Often teams up in winter like tits to search for food and their classic finch beak is designed for picking seeds out of teasels and thistles.

 Size: 12 cm.

 When to spot: All year round, although some migrate south as far as Spain in winter.

 Diet: Seeds, seeds and more seeds!

 On the table: Nyjer seeds and sunflower hearts.

 Breeding and nesting: Grass and moss cup-shaped nests in trees.

Greenfinch

These zoom and flash around the garden and I might say unimaginatively, 'oh look, how wonderful it's a greenfinch!' The male has more yellow all round than the female. Their numbers have been up and down over the years, one reason being an outbreak of trichomonosis (a disease carried by parasites that stops them feeding properly).

 Size: 15 cm.

 When to spot: All year round.

 Diet: Seeds and insects.

 On the table: Peanuts and black sunflower seeds.

 Breeding and nesting: Grass/moss nests in trees.

chaffinch

Chaffinches are common in the UK and Ireland. The male is a dandy with a blue-grey crown, brown back and pink breast. Females are brown, similar but less streaky than female house sparrows, and have white shoulder patches. Often seen hopping around under bird tables rather than on them.

 Size: 15 cm.

 When to spot: All year round.

 Diet: Insects and seeds.

 On the table: Sunflowers seeds and hearts.

 Breeding and nesting: Mossy nests in trees and shrubs.

House Sparrow

When I was a kid, sparrows were widespread and abundant, often hopping under or onto a table looking for any dropped scraps. Their numbers dropped by a staggering 71% between 1977 and 2008 in both rural and urban populations and, although stabilising, they are still at risk. They are chatty and friendly, tend to breed near humans and have made homes all over the world.

 Size: 15 cm.

 When to spot: All year round.

 Diet: Adults eat seeds, fats and grain and feed their young solely on insects and caterpillars.

 On the table: Sunflower seeds, suet, mealworms.

 Breeding and nesting: Compact cup shape from moss, grass and feathers in trees and walls.

Robin

I know I'm not supposed to have a favourite, but the robin is simply adorable, and gardeners know just how friendly they get as they follow us around the garden singing away. They are very territorial, chasing off intruders. Males and females both have red breasts, juveniles are golden brown and speckled.

 Size: 13 cm.

 When to spot: All year round.

 Diet: Worms, seeds, fruit, insects, and invertebrates.

 On the table: Mealworms and sunflower hearts.

 Breeding and nesting: Varied. Made up of grass, leaves and moss in tree holes, bird boxes, ivy, etc.

song thrush

Song thrushes have a wonderfully lyrical song, repeating phrases in search of a number one hit! Brown with lighter breast streaked with brown. Seen hopping through the garden with its head on one side. Sadly, they have been in decline over recent years.

 Size: 22 cm.

 When to spot: Year round.

 Diet: Smashes snails against a stone, worms, seeds.

 On the table: Not that keen on feeding stations but will often eat sunflower hearts, suet and mealworms off the ground.

 Breeding and nesting: Grass, twig and mud nests in trees, shrubs and climbers, often low down.

Dunnock

Looks similar to a sparrow (hence its other name of hedge sparrow), brown with dark streaks, but its beak is narrower and more pointed. Usually seen on its own and shuffles around flicking its wings. Feeds on the ground.

 Size: 15 cm.

 When to spot: All year round.

 Diet: Insects and seeds.

 On the table: Tend not to use tables so may be spotted in winter picking up seeds and suet.

 Breeding and nesting: Moss and grass nests in hedges and shrubs.

Wren

Delightful little creatures. Small and brown with distinct upturned tails. For their size, they blast out a pretty loud warble. Quite tricky to see but spotted hurling leaves, mulch and compost around in search of insects.

 Size: 10 cm.

 When to spot: All year round.

 Diet: Insects and seeds.

 On the table: Mealworms are their favourite, but they also go for peanut hearts, suet and fruit.

 Breeding and nesting: In trees, shrubs, hedges, sheds and outbuildings.

Jay: Most colourful member of the crow family. Quite shy, screaming call and loves to bury acorns for 'Ron' (that's later on!).

Magpie: Common and quite mischievous. Large black and white birds that feed on just about anything, including carrion.

Green woodpecker: Red head and green wings, seen hopping around on lawns looking for grubs and insects.

Spotted woodpecker: The common garden one: black, white and red. Drums on trees in spring.

Collared dove: Pale pink-grey with distinctive black collar. Often seen on their own.

Pied wagtail: Long tail that wags up and down, black, white and grey.

Starling: Blackbird-like with greenish back. Hangs out in gangs, very clever but sometimes seen as a nuisance.

Wood pigeon: Our most common pigeon. Grey back and white neck patch and recognisable 'coo coo' call.

water

Birds need water for both drinking and bathing in, especially in winter (when other sources may be frozen) and summer (when they may have dried out altogether). Most birds drink by dipping their beaks in and then throwing their heads back to swallow, so need somewhere to stand on the edge. Bathing is a key element too. It keeps their important feathers in good shape; wetting them loosens the dirt and makes them easier to preen. A simple birdbath will do the trick but make sure to clean it regularly and change the water. You can use some well-diluted washing-up liquid but make sure to rinse it off thoroughly. Stop it freezing in winter by pouring warm water onto it or placing a light ball in it that will gently move around and do the job too.

Bird box for small birds (tits and sparrows etc.)

Materials and tools

A plank of sustainably sourced wood (FSC registered, non-pressure treated wood) around 1.4 m long x 15 cm wide x 1.5 cm thick (you can use thicker but may need to adjust measurements). Thickness is important for insulation in cold weather, reduced heat in summer and to stop it warping. Pine is fine but won't last forever; exterior grade plywood is a good choice or a hardwood like oak is ideal and will last many years.

- Pencil and tape measure.

- Saw.

- Drill.

- Nails and screws.

- Hole cutter or jigsaw.

- An offcut of waterproof rubber.

- Oh, and a ladder for putting it up!

How to build your bird box:

1 Measure and cut the wood like in the picture.

2 Cut a hole 3.2 cm in diameter (use a hole cutter or drill a hole and use the jigsaw). If a perfect circles is a problem, square is fine.

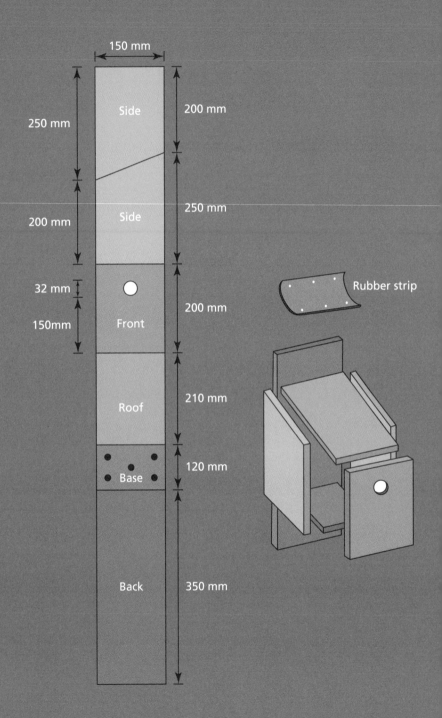

150 mm

Side

200 mm

250 mm

Side

200 mm

250 mm

32 mm

Front

150mm

200 mm

Roof

210 mm

Base

120 mm

Back

350 mm

Rubber strip

3 Nail the sides, back and front together around the base.

4 Attach the roof using screws so you can unscrew them later to clean if required.

5 Nail down a strip of rubber (or plastic membrane or sliced open old bicycle inner tube) over the edge where the roof meets the back plate as a water seal.

6 Decorate your box if you wish. Paint it only with water-based paints and don't paint around the entrance hole or the inside as birds may peck it. Greys and greens tend to blend in with the garden best and won't put off any birds.

7 Drill holes in the back plate for fixings (this depends on what you're fixing onto), either using Rawlplugs® and screws into walls or screws into fences, or galvanised wire around trees, but check annually to make sure it doesn't cut into the bark.

8 Site around 3 m off the ground (be careful on ladders). Site in shade facing away from the prevailing wind and rain (so generally facing northerly, easterly or south-easterly) with easy access for flight and away from predators. A blank wall at 3 m high may not look that appealing but is usually a safe spot.

Types of bird feeders

Peanut feeders are made of steel mesh. The mesh size needs to be around 6 mm. Large enough to prevent beak damage and small enough to prevent large pieces being taken.

Seed feeders are tubular transparent containers with holes designed for sunflower seeds and seed mixes labelled as 'feeder seed'.

Nyjer seed is smaller and needs a special seed feeder. Goldfinches love them!

Home-made devices: Half-coconuts, fir cones and the like can be filled or smothered with fat, bird cake, etc. and can be hung from your bird table, a tree or bracket on a wall.

Warning: Peanuts and fat balls are often sold in nylon mesh bags. Always take the product out first and never put the bag out directly as they can trap birds' feet and cause broken legs.

Feeds

Birds used to be fed mainly in winter when food was scarce, but these days year-round feeding is seen as a good idea as it gives them energy when breeding, bringing up their young and perhaps gives them extra energy to source food for themselves. If you only feed at certain times, go for winter and spring. There's a lot of different feeds out there to choose from and they do vary in quality (some are bulked up with grain, etc.)

Seed mixes: Look for mixes that contain high proportions of crushed peanuts, maize, and sunflower seeds and hearts.

Sunflowers seeds: Choose black seed over striped where possible as the oil content is higher. Sunflower hearts are even better as no energy is lost removing the husk.

Nyjer seed: Tiny black seed high in oils (will need a special feeder).

Peanuts: High in energy. Use in feeders only. Poor-quality peanuts can carry the aflatoxin fungus, which kills birds if they eat it, so only buy aflatoxin-free from a reputable supplier.

Suet/fat: For winter feeding. Fat balls, or make your own with 50% beef fat and 50% mixed seeds in a tuna can and place in the fridge before turning out as solid shape. Don't use regular cooking fat.

Mealworms: A fine source of protein and calories during the breeding season. Bought live or dried (which can be rehydrated).

other sources of food

Tinned pet food: Often used in dry summers when earthworms aren't plentiful. Don't use dry biscuits.

Potatoes: Baked, roasted and mashed potatoes (with or without real fat) are fine for birds.

Pastry: made with real fat either cooked or uncooked makes a good feed.

what not to feed birds

- Salty items, such as salted peanuts, crisps and bacon, should be avoided.

- Anything that could choke a bird, such as whole peanuts, lumps of hard fat and dried bread.

- Any mouldy or stale food. Bread isn't harmful to birds but fills them up and has very low protein and fat content so may be detrimental.

- Milk. A bird's gut is not designed to digest milk and it can cause serious stomach upset and even death.

plants for birds

Plants for shelter, berries, fruit or seed offer multiple benefits and not only to birds, but other forms of wildlife too. The key is to get a varied mix of plants. In the autumn and into the winter, many birds rely on the berries, haws or hips, which can be extremely nutritious, containing high levels of vitamins, antioxidants and raw energy. Some birds get most of their food from autumn and winter berries anyway, but if the ground is frozen hard or other food sources are scarce, other birds will compete and so reduce the available bounty, making survival tougher all round. What we plant can make all the difference. Here are some fine choices for the small to medium-sized garden.

Trees

Snowy mespilus (*Amelanchier*): Early to flower and stunning autumn colour and the small, almost black fruit is a favourite with birds. Everyone's happy!

Alder (*Alnus glutinosa*): British native and ideal for wet and heavy soils, providing catkins in spring and cones in winter.

Bird cherry (*Prunus padus*):
Fruiting cherries are beautiful in flower and produce delicious fruit that you're likely to compete with birds for! Our native bird cherry is often seen in hedgerows, grown as shrubs  and is a great all-round wildlife tree. Their pea-sized fruit is loved by birds but not us – argument over!

Crab apple (*Malus*): Fabulous garden trees with white flowers in spring, fiery autumn foliage and an abundance of persisting fruit. 'Red sentinel' has clusters of small red rounded fruit, while 'John  Downie' has masses of larger orange-red fruit.

Hawthorn (*Crataegus*): Thorny number that makes a great nesting site and its haws, which are rich in antioxidants, stay on the tree until February or March.

Holly (*Ilex*): Brilliant wildlife tree as its prickly leaves offer protection on the tree as well as on the ground for many creatures when they drop. Only female plants produce berries (so make sure or  buy when in berry) and need a male nearby to ensure pollination.

Hazel (*Corylus avellana*): Another great all-rounder for wildlife across the seasons. The nuts are eaten by woodpeckers, nuthatches, tits, wood pigeons and jays and coppiced trees provide shelter for ground-nesting birds.

Rowan and ornamental ash (*Sorbus*): Fabulous all-round ornamental garden trees. 'Aria' has red berries, 'Joseph Rock' has small yellow berries, *Sorbus cashmiriana* has white berries, while 'Pink Pagoda'

has, yup, pink berries. Pick any colour you want. The birds love them all.

Silver birch (*Betula*): Great for insects as many caterpillars, sawflies and moths live on them so bring in the birds to feed. The seeds in the catkins are eaten too.

Yew (*Taxus baccata*): Dense evergreen tree often grown as a hedge, providing good cover. The red berries have a fleshy skin that is eaten by birds.

Shrubs

Cotoneaster: Many varieties for all kinds of situations. (*C.* x *Wateri*) wall shrubs (*C. cornubia*) and ground cover (*C. horizontales* and *C. dammeri*), to name a few. They all have masses of bright red berries that birds adore.

Roses: If you don't deadhead roses, most will develop hips. Dog roses (*rosa canina*), beach roses (*rosa rugosa*) and one of my favourites, *rosa glauca,* are all fine choices but there are so many more!

Elder (*Sambucus nigra*): Great all-rounder providing shelter, insects and berries. If it gets out of control, cut it hard back in late winter to get it back into shape.

Mahonia: Bombproof plants that'll grow anywhere. Spiky architectural leaves, cheery yellow, scented upright blooms in deep winter followed by deep purple berries, which nicely bridges the gap for birds until spring.

Firethorn (*Pyracantha*): Prolific and reliable thorny, berrying, evergreen shrubs that tick a lot of boxes and can be trained into rather elaborate wall shrubs. Make sure not to prune off any flower buds  after flowering as it will lead to less fruit. Available in red, orange and yellow berrying varieties.

Guelder rose (*Viburnum opulus*): Snowball-like flowers in spring, fabulous autumn colour and bunches of translucent red berries. Many other deciduous and evergreen viburnums berry well too.

Japanese barberry (*Berberis thunbergia*): Deciduous shrub with intense deep-red foliage and yellow flowers in the autumn. Red, smooth, hip-like fruit appears in the autumn, which many birds enjoy and  the prickly thorns provide a relatively safe nesting site.

Heavenly bamboo (*Nandina domestica 'firepower'*): Exotic-looking plant from the Far East with plenty of deep sealing-wax red berries held high in a spray above the fine cut foliage. Birds can sit on the top and chomp away.

Fatsia japonica: Tough, evergreen shrub with large, glossy deep-cut leaves. Clusters of persistent black fruit follow the panicles of creamy white flowers. Ideal for an exotic style garden and happy in deep shade.

Other fine shrubs for birds include callicarpa, aucuba, skimmia and buckthorn.

climbers

Honeysuckle (*Lonicera periclymenum*): Scented flowers in summer followed by clusters of red berries into the winter. Creates a perfect site for nesting birds too, but not to be encouraged if cats can easily prey.

English ivy (*Hedera helix*): One of the best winter food sources for birds. They persist well into deep winter when they may be the only food around. If you can, let one romp away, they are fabulous all-rounders for

wildlife (flowers for bees, berries and evergreen cover for nesting birds).

Clematis are great for nesting birds and varieties such as *Clematis tangutica* develop fluffy 'old man's beard' seed heads, ideal for nesting material.

Perennials can be grown for their seeds and fluffy seed heads for nesting. Some host insects too, which birds will feed on:

scabious (field scabious and devil's-bit scabious)

greater knapweed

evening primrose

lemon balm

teasel

sunflowers (helianthus)

yarrow

michaelmas dasies

honesty

globe thistle

bugs, beetles and other insects

These days, we call many insects 'bugs' (I'm sure it's an American thing and don't remember it from my childhood). Technically 'true bugs' belong to the Hemiptera order, of which there around 2,000 wide-ranging species in the UK, including shield bugs, leafhoppers, aphids and pond skaters. Plenty can be found in your garden and a broad mix of planting, a pond, some long grass and some nooks and crannies to overwinter in (getting the hang of this wildlife gardening now?) will create the ideal habitat for them. Don't try to control them, this is what makes gardening with wildlife in mind perhaps different to conventional gardening. Many are predated on and bring in animals further up the food chain so are fundamental to the ecological balance, so the more the merrier. Aphids (such as greenfly, blackfly and black bean aphids) are perhaps the most commonly unloved and sprayed bugs, viewed as 'garden pests', but they are a staple diet of many others, including beneficial ladybirds (and their larvae), hoverfly larvae, as well as tits and sparrows. It's a no-brainer in my opinion: let them all get on with it, fighting it out in the jungle that is your garden, and a balance will be found.

Beetles

Beetles are different from bugs in that they have toughened forewings for protection and bite and cut their food, whereas true bugs suck sap and plant juices. We have around 4,500 species of beetles in the UK, which make up around 40% of our insect species. Many are in decline thanks to the common story of pesticides, modern farming, and habitat loss and fragmentation. They range from around 1 mm in size to the largest, the stag beetle, which can grow to 8 cm in length. Not all will visit our gardens, but a wide range will if given the right conditions.

Here are some ways to identify the beetles in your nature garden:

Cockchafer (May bug): Around 2.5 cm long. Their body is a rusty brown, with antennae that fan out and are used to find a mate. They appear in spring, are attracted to lights and make a low buzzing noise when in flight. Their larvae are large, creamy-white grubs known as rook worms for obvious reasons.

Ladybird:
Much loved and easily recognisable. Most have bright red wing cases and black spots, but some are black, yellow or white-brown

(and sometimes striped). The most common are the two-spot and seven-spot. They hibernate in cracks and leaf litter and I've found them in dense plants, emerging in April to mate and munch on aphids.

Stag beetle:
Awesome looking large beetles with antler-shaped mandibles. They are harmless to us. Males have a red tinge and females are shiny black and smaller

and without the antlers. They spend most of their life underground as larvae feeding on dead wood and rotting tree roots and emerge in May for a few weeks to mate.

Violet ground beetle: Up to 35 mm long with black smooth oval wing cases with violet edges. Nocturnal hunters, they don't fly but run (pretty fast!). The larvae are meat eaters, feeding on worms, slugs and other insects.

Thick-legged flower beetle (the swollen-thighed beetle and the false oil beetle): Males have a metallic green body with distinctly thickened hind legs. It's a pollinator of many open flowers including cow parsley and ox-eye daisies and the larvae are well-hidden within the dry stems of plants where they feed and grow before emerging to become adults.

other insects in your garden

Garden ant: They farm aphids for their sweet honeydew and go for anything sweet like rotting fruit and nectar. Every year, masses of flying ants are seen as they leave their nests in search of a mate (big feeding day for birds!) and after mating, only the females survive, lose their wings and start a new colony.

Damselfly: I adore these blue, green and black beauties as they fly around my pond from June to September in search of midges, flies and mosquitoes. They sometimes form a heart shape when mating (aww ...) and lay eggs in pond plants just below the water's surface. Make a pond and they'll turn up.

Earwig: Brown slender insects with distinctive pincers on their rear end. Okay, so they munch a garden plant here and there (especially dahlias) but they predate on aphids too. Love a log stack and stone crevices.

Field grasshopper: Beige-brown in colour. In summer you may hear them chirping (to attract a mate) as they rub their back legs together. They lay their eggs in the soil and live in long grass and feed on it.

Earthworm: Worms are fantastic for our gardens, composting organic waste and drawing it down into the soil, aerating it as they go. If you have imported some new sterile topsoil, buy a bag of worms online to speed up the process. Birds and hedgehogs find them particularly delicious.

Spiders: There's a host of spiders you may see in our gardens, including the garden spider, which has many colour forms including brown, yellow-green and orange and which spins spiral webs along hedges and between tall stems. The four-spot orb weaver is the UK's largest spider and is broader and rounder, with four indented dimples on its abdomen, usually outlined with four white spots.

Attracting bugs, beetles and other insects into your garden

- Never use pesticides and leave aphids alone as they will attract predators.

- Grow a good range of plants across the season, including leafy and flowering plants, climbers, a patch of nettles and some umbels (like angelica, fennel and orlaya).

- Create some areas with dense planting.

- Make a log pile or bug hotel.

- Make a compost heap.

- Leave dead wood on trees and any tree stumps in the ground.

- Live with weeds.

- Regularly mulch borders for insect cover.

hedgehogs

Hedgehogs are wonderful creatures, once a common sight in the countryside and our gardens. The decline in their population over recent years is frightening – an estimated reduction in their population of 50% since 2000 – and sadly they're now on the red list for British mammals and in danger of extinction. Their decline is likely due to a combination of factors including habitat loss (hedgerows and field margins) and fragmentation, increase in road traffic and paved areas in gardens. The largest decline, perhaps surprisingly, is in rural, not urban, areas, yet it shows that if we can garden in towns and suburbs with them in mind it's hopefully not too late and we can make a significant difference. Hedgehogs are nocturnal, meat eaters and mostly solitary, yet come together in spring to mate. Their nests can be quite large and made of moss, grass leaves and other debris and found at the bottom of hedgerows, brambles, compost heaps and garden sheds.

Hedgehog diet

They eat caterpillars, beetles, slugs, worms, earwigs, etc. You can feed them too, which is especially welcome in autumn as they build up fat reserves before hibernation or during dry summers when food and water are scarce. Leave food out, such as meaty cat or dog food or cat biscuits and some water in a shallow dish. Never feed them bread (low in energy, so worthless) or milk (they are lactose intolerant; it could kill them).

make your garden safe for hedgehogs

Water: Yes, I've encouraged you all to introduce water into the garden to attract wildlife. Hedgehogs are fairly good swimmers but tire quickly and don't fare well with steep or slippery sides. Ensure they can get in and out of ponds easily by having some gently sloping sides or some wire mesh or a plank they can scramble up.

Dogs: Dogs can be a real problem for hedgehogs, especially if they're territorial. The two tend not to be compatible.

Roads: Just as we want to open up safe 'wildlife corridors', if your garden has direct access onto a road then consider what you can do. Perhaps block this dangerous route but only if you can offer any hedgehogs another, as they hate to be boxed in.

Compost heaps: They may hibernate in your compost heap, so be careful. Leave turning till late March/April to ensure they have moved on.

Slug pellets and pesticides: These can kill hedgehogs directly, but also get into the food chain they rely on. Avoid altogether and talk to your neighbours about refraining too.

Strimming lawns: Pay extra attention in case a hedgehog is hiding out in the long grass, as they often do in the daytime.

Fences: (see wildlife corridors above.)

making a hedgehog house

You can make a hedgehog house from scratch or adapt a wooden crate or box (a large wine box is ideal. Any excuse, eh?). The main thing is it's sturdy and dry. Make sure the lid can come off for cleaning so leave it unfixed or use hinges. Do not treat wood with non-water based preservatives and only treat the outside of the box if you want.

Here's a simple design:

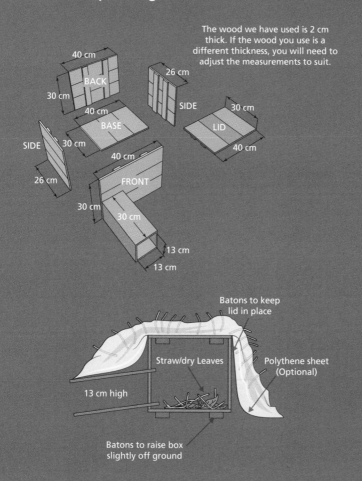

The wood we have used is 2 cm thick. If the wood you use is a different thickness, you will need to adjust the measurements to suit.

40 cm
BACK
30 cm
40 cm
BASE
SIDE
30 cm
26 cm
SIDE
30 cm
30 cm
LID
40 cm
40 cm
FRONT
30 cm
30 cm
13 cm
13 cm

Batons to keep lid in place
Straw/dry Leaves
Polythene sheet (Optional)
13 cm high
Batons to raise box slightly off ground

You could also make one just by placing old bricks for the sides and entrance tunnel and simply place a piece of stone or some plywood over the top. Put some dry grass or straw inside first and then you can cover with a polythene sheet and then pile soil and leaves over the top if you wish to help hide it better, but the hedgehogs won't really care what it looks like from the outside. Straw and leaves left outside may be taken in.

Siting

Place in a quiet spot, preferably against a bank, wall, or fence and hopefully one will turn up. Face the entrance away from cold north or northeast winds.

Clean if you want (not particularly necessary) in late March/early April after winter use. Never clean if a hedgehog's living in there. How do you know? Put something light and small in the entrance (a small piece of cork?) and if it moves overnight, bingo!, it probably means one's checked in! Wait for them to vacate and then take the lid off and clean using hot water and a scrubbing brush, let it dry fully before adding in more straw or dry grass and placing the lid back on.

amphibians

We have seven species of amphibians in the whole of the UK and they are extremely important wetland animals. They are predators (mainly feeding on pest insects, slugs and snails), yet are prey themselves too, making a tasty meal for birds and even hedgehogs. It's all a part of the cycle of life, I'm afraid! If you have some amphibians or can attract some into your garden, it means your space is acting as a vital resource and providing the depth of habitat and range of food for them to survive in.

common frog

This is our most common amphibian, found throughout Britain and Ireland, although its numbers are in decline through habitat loss and disease. It's a regular visitor to garden ponds and a gardener's friend (by keeping slugs and snails at bay).

It grows to around 13 cm long with smooth skin and long legs used for hopping or jumping (it doesn't walk). It can be found in a wide range of colours, usually olive-green or brown but may sometimes be red or yellow with dark patches on its back and a dark mask behind the eye. It can lighten or darken its skin to match its surroundings.

Common frogs don't technically hibernate but spend the winter under rocks or in compost heaps and underwater buried in mud and vegetation until they emerge in spring to breed. Common frogs deposit 'rafts' of spawn from late winter to late summer and each clump can often contain up to 2,000 eggs.

common toad

Its Latin name is *Bufo bufo*, which I think is far cooler and suits it better. It is widespread and common across mainland UK and well known for migrating en masse to breeding ponds. It can live up to 12 years and munches on slugs, snails, insects and spiders, and larger ones may even eat slow worms, small grass snakes and mice. To protect itself from predators, it secretes a toxin from its skin and puffs itself up to look all, well, Bufo bufo!

The common toad varies in colour from dark brown, grey and olive-green to sandy and it has a distinctly squat body and warty skin. Females are around 13 cm long and larger than the males. It walks or crawls rather than hops so it's easy to distinguish from a frog. Toadlets hatch from strings of spawn. Long strings of spawn are laid around aquatic plants with two rows of eggs per string.

The common toad tends to breed in larger, deeper ponds than common frogs, but is a frequent visitor to gardens. It hibernates through winter under log piles, stones and sometimes in old flowerpots so be careful when tidying up. On the first warm, damp evening of the year, around mid-February, it heads back to its breeding pond and lays its eggs.

Smooth newt

Also known as the 'common newt' and the one you're most likely to see in your garden pond.

They grow up to 10 cm long and their skin colour varies in shades of grey or brown, with a yellow or orange belly. They usually have black spots or blotches on their undersides and, on land, their skin takes on a velvety appearance and they're sometimes mistaken for lizards. Males have a wavy crest along their back during the breeding season.

Smooth newts eat small crustaceans like shrimps, molluscs and tadpoles when in the water. They spend winter sheltering under rocks, in compost heaps or buried down in mud. Occasionally, they'll overwinter in ponds. Males perform groovy courtship dances to attract the females and then the greyish-brown eggs are deposited individually on the leaves of pond plants. The larvae have feathery gills that help distinguish them from frog and toad tadpoles.

palmate newt

Looks remarkably similar to the smooth newt and although widespread is less likely to be spotted in gardens (but may be). Its natural habitat is shallow ponds on acidic heathlands and moorlands, so it's more commonly found in Scotland, Wales and southern England. During breeding, the males grow distinctive black webbing on their back feet (hence its 'palmate' name).

Great crested newt

The UK's population of the great crested newt is internationally important as they're under threat from habitat loss and farming practices. Their distribution is widespread in lowland England and Wales but very patchy. A garden pond may just attract some and help save their species.

They are our biggest newt, around 15 cm long, with warty skin almost black in colour and spotted flanks and a striking, orange belly. Males have a white line on their tail, females a yellow one. Males develop a wavy crest along the body and tail during breeding season.

They breed in the spring in (ideally large) ponds with plenty of vegetation (and no fish), spending the rest of the year feeding in woodland, hedgerows and marshes, so make sure there's plenty of cover nearby if your garden's big enough. They hibernate underground among tree roots and in old walls. During the mating season, males do an amazing dance standing on their front legs, arch their back and wave their tail around as if they're body popping to the latest tunes! The female lays roughly 300 eggs, individually folded inside the leaves of aquatic plants.

Protection
Great crested newts are protected under UK law, making it illegal to kill, injure, capture, disturb or sell them, or to damage or destroy their habitats.

Attracting amphibians into your garden

A wildlife pond is the best way and it'll bring in all manner of wildlife too. See the chapter on wildlife ponds and include the following:

- At least one side of the pool should gently slope up to land to enable the young to leave the water once the tadpole stage is over. If the pond has steep sides, have a ramp covered in chicken wire.

- Small amphibians are prey to birds so growing plants around the pool will provide cover.

- When in the pond, frogs and toads will need a point above the water on which to rest and breathe. Place a few rocks or logs half in and half out of the water.

- Allow new ponds to become colonised naturally by amphibians that are likely to be present in the area already (they'll turn up). Never transfer spawn or tadpoles from other ponds as it runs the risk of spreading diseases, such as 'red leg disease' of frogs.

- Attract newts (the most aquatic of amphibians) by letting grass grow over the pond edge into the water.

- Newts use narrow-leaved water plants on which to lay their eggs, placing each egg between a folded leaf. Introduce marginal and submerged native plants like water mint (*mentha aquatica*), brooklime (*veronica beccabunga*) and water forget-me-not (*myosotis scorpioides*).

- Fish will eat spawn, tadpoles and other pond life so don't put any fish into ponds for amphibians.

- Frogs and newts often overwinter in the bottom of ponds in the autumn, so avoid cleaning out in winter.

- Many amphibians seek sheltered places away from water where they shelter until the following spring so provide shelter with log piles, a stone pile and be careful as they may be in compost heaps and under hedges and shrubs too.

bats

Bats are amazing creatures. We have 17 species in the UK and the more common species often visit gardens to feed in them, or may shelter in them during the daytime if conditions are right. They are seen as rural animals, yet many will also be found in towns and cities. Sadly, like so much of our wildlife, they're in trouble. They get a bad press but don't build nests and their poo is good for the garden and smells of ... nothing at all. Oh, and they aren't blind either, they have small eyes with sensitive vision, which helps them see in night-time conditions. They don't have the sharp and colourful vision we have but don't need it as most use echolocation to find their food.

Here are the ones you are most likely to see in your garden between March and November (maybe others if you're lucky).

Common and soprano pipistrelle: Pipistrelles are the most common bat in the UK, small (around 4–5 cm long) and have brown fur, pale undersides and almost black ears and wings. These two are very closely related, almost impossible to tell apart without a bat detector (a handheld device that converts their echolocation ultrasound to audible frequency 'clicks and smacks' – you may want to invest in a basic one for around £50–£100).

Brown long-eared bat: Second most common bat in the UK. Yup, you guessed it, long ears (seriously long, about the same length as their body) and brown (quite light brown, actually) fur! Grows to around 8 cm. Very quiet call. Their hearing makes them fine hunters in woodland areas.

Daubenton's bat: Named in honour of eighteenth-century French naturalist Louis-Jean-Marie Daubenton, they're around 5–6 cm long with a wingspan of around 20 cm. They have black-brown fur and a sweet pink face. They're often seen swooping low across water where they pick insects off the surface with their tail or large feet. Skilful, eh?

Food

Bats eat all kinds of insects including moths, mosquitoes, midges and other flies, mayflies, some beetles, caddisflies, lacewings and other nocturnal insects. They mostly catch insects in mid-air on the wing, using echolocation to home in on their prey.

City and garden lights

Although you may see them feeding on insects flying around lights at night in summer (such as moths), artificial lighting is generally viewed as negative for them.

Shelter and habitats

During daytime, bats shelter in dark places such as in hollow trees, roof spaces, under roof tiles, in loose bark on trees or in splits in the trunks. Linear features such as hedges and streams are important as feeding areas and navigation pathways as they travel between roosting sites and feeding areas.

Make your garden more bat-friendly

- Grow plants for a range of insects and include some for moths and night-flying insects (see the butterflies and moths chapter).

- Ponds are fabulous for attracting insects that bats feed on. What, you haven't got a pond yet? How many reasons do you need?

- Compost heaps, log stacks, etc., are great and any other features where insects breed for them to feed on.

shelter

- Bats generally find their own places to shelter and if you see them roosting, try your best not to disturb them. Bat boxes (see making a bat box below) can be bought or made and sited on tree trunks or walls of buildings.

- Bats like warm, sheltered places in summer. When placing bat boxes (unlike bird boxes), choose locations with a sunny southerly or westerly aspect and avoid draughty spots or placing above doors or windows where they may get disturbed.

- Retain any old trees or large shrubs in the garden with cavities, splits in the trunk or loose bark as long as they're safe.

making a bat box

What you'll need:

A plank of untreated sawn timber at least 1.2 m long, 10 cm wide and thick (minimum 15 mm to keep them insulated, this design is for a 20 mm thick plank). If it's too smooth bats can't get a grip, so rough it up both sides a bit with a saw so they can grab on.

- Tape measure and pencil.

- Saw.

- Hammer.

- Drill.

- Nails.

How to:

1 Mark the wood with a pencil, according to the diagram, and then cut it into the sections.

2 Make a groove in the back plate by carefully cutting across with a saw.

3 Nail (or glue) all the pieces together as shown in the diagram, making the joints as airtight as possible.

4 Make lid by fixing a strip so it sits nice and snug in the groove.

Siting it

Site it a minimum of 3 metres from the ground on the trunk of a tree. Drill two holes onto top section of back plate, use galvanised wire, feed through and fix well (but check for cutting into bark regularly) or drill one hole and fix with rawplug and screws under the eaves of the house in an easily accessible spot and away from artificial light. A sunny southerly or westerly aspect protected from winds and draughts. They hate a cold draught, don't blame them so do I!

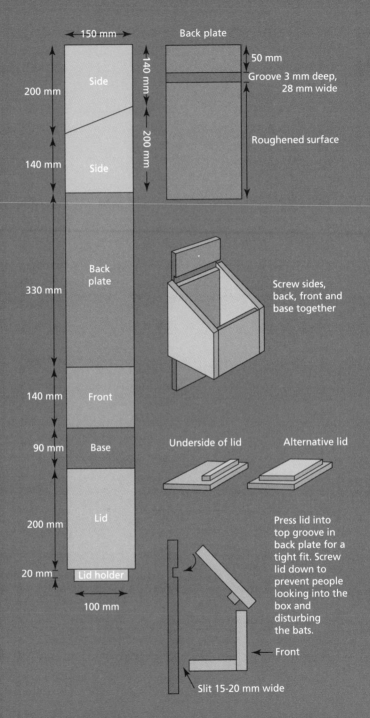

← 150 mm →

Side

200 mm

140 mm

Side

140 mm

200 mm

Back plate

50 mm

Groove 3 mm deep, 28 mm wide

Roughened surface

Back plate

330 mm

Screw sides, back, front and base together

Front

140 mm

90 mm

Base

Underside of lid

Alternative lid

Lid

200 mm

Press lid into top groove in back plate for a tight fit. Screw lid down to prevent people looking into the box and disturbing the bats.

20 mm

Lid holder

100 mm

← Front

Slit 15-20 mm wide

bees and other pollinators

I'm rather proud that there are bees buzzing nearly all year round in my garden. When I see and hear them, I know I'm doing my little, but important, bit for a group of insects that are in serious trouble. Their decline over recent years has been well documented but becomes increasingly worrying. We only have around 276 bee species (out of around 16,000 worldwide) in the UK and have already lost 13 species in the UK altogether (another 35 are currently at risk). This is down to a combination of factors (habitat loss, climate change, diseases and invasive species) but the biggest factor is unrelenting modern farming methods and the mass use of pesticides, especially neonicotinoids.

When most of us think of bees, we tend to think of the fluffy bumblebee or the smaller honeybee, but the majority species-wise are collectively called 'solitary bees', which don't live in social groups. While some look like bees, others look like wasps or flies and some are so small you may never see them to see exactly what they look like!

When it comes to helping bees out, every garden, allotment, roof terrace, pot, container, window box and unmanicured lawn (ideally with some clover in it!) counts. City and suburban gardens are just as important as rural spaces; in fact, honey produced in city hives is notoriously deeper in flavour due to the varied palette of plants the bees have visited and harvested nectar from. Anyone who grows edibles will know how important it is for their crops to be pollinated (it's estimated that a third of all our food is pollinated by bees) but by growing them in the first place, the pollinators are benefitting for their survival too; it's a two-way street.

Honeybees are mostly kept in managed hives and are estimated to pollinate between 5 and 15% of the UK's insect-pollinated crops. That leaves between 85 to 95% of the UK's insect-pollinated crops relying on other wild pollinators, including other species of bee, but also moths, butterflies, hoverflies, flies, wasps and beetles.

These are the most common types of bees you may see in your garden.

Bumblebees (around 25 Bombus species in the UK)

- A bumblebee nest will have between 50 and 400 worker bees and are busiest in summer.

- In most cases, only young, fertile female bumblebees (queens) overwinter.

- Most species have queens that burrow into the soil to overwinter, emerging on sunny days in spring.

- In spring, the queens search for nest sites, often choosing tunnels made by mice or rodents.

- The queen sets about laying larvae in early spring. Once they become adult worker bumblebees, they collect nectar and pollen, allowing the queen to remain in the nest and continue laying eggs.

- In mid to late summer, male bumblebees and next year's queens are produced.

- By late summer, bumblebee nests are in decline, with the old queen, workers and males all dying.

Solitary bees (Andrena, Lasioglossum and other species)

- There are around 250 species of solitary bee in Britain.

- Unlike bumble and honeybees, solitary bees do not have a worker caste.

- Each female constructs and provides food for her nest, then dies before the next generation emerges.

- Despite being solitary, some are pretty sociable with other nests nearby.

- Soil-nesting bees produce conical heaps of soil above the nest tunnels where excavated soil has been deposited. You've probably seen them.

- Other solitary bees make their nests in hollow plant stems, soft rotten wood, and beetle holes in dead wood. The leaf-cutter bee makes its nest from, yes you guessed it ... leaves!

- Most solitary bees are active in spring or summer, although the ivy bee has become widespread since it was found in Britain in 2001 (the adults visit ivy flowers in autumn).

Honeybee (Apis mellifera)

This is a single species that lives in colonies of up to 60,000 and produces honey. Most are maintained by beekeepers in hives.

- Each hive has a single queen bee whose role is to lay eggs and organise the colony.

- There will be several hundred male honeybees (drones).

- Most in the hive are infertile female worker bees that do all the work by going out to gather nectar and pollen, care for the larvae and build the combs to store honey.

Hoverflies

Hoverflies may look rather like bees and wasps but are not related. There are around 280 species, from around 4 mm to 16 mm long and they zoom around the garden and hover with control in a mesmerizing way. They're clever too: although they can't sting, they often mimic predators (both looking and acting like them) in a bid to be left well alone. As well as being top pollinators, they're great for munching on aphids too as part of your biological pest control, so the more welcome you can make them, the better. They lay their eggs close to aphid colonies, a little like living next door to a supermarket! They're relatively short-lived – from a few days to a few weeks – and have a weakness for umbellifers like fennel, cow parsley and wild carrot.

what we can do for pollinators

Well, the good news is that gardening for pollinators is easy and will only add depth to your plot, while making it more beautiful to look at too, a win-win! Planting for them will bring them in initially and they will hopefully look to stay, nest and breed so it's also about making habitats with them in mind.

It's not only about the nectar-rich plants in your garden; pollen is also an important source of protein for bees and makes them stronger and less prone to disease. There are hundreds of nectar and pollen-rich plants to choose from and combine together to make up a pollinator-friendly garden. The basic rule when choosing plants is to look for open flowers where nectar and pollen are easily accessed. Daisy, bell-shaped flowers, umbellifers (like fennel) and open flowers like buttercups are always a favourite. Many modern garden centre plants are highly bred hybrids grown for specific requirements such as dwarfing, larger blooms, different colours or double blooms (which are closed and almost impossible for pollinators to access). As a plant is bred and hybridised further, it loses its nectar and pollen content (and scent), and because they're likely to have been grown by vegetative cuttings, won't need to be pollinated to survive, so lose those qualities further. Look for plants as close to the original species as possible – often wonderful cottage garden plants – and include some wildflowers and herbs wherever possible.

The Royal Horticultural Society (RHS) has a 'Plants for Pollinators' list that gets updated every year, which is well worth checking out.

Great spring and summer plants for pollinators

Trees: Apples and crab apples, cherries, hawthorn, holly.

Shrubs and climbers: Lavenders, cotoneaster, lilac, clematis, honeysuckle, roses (single or semi-double), jasmine.

Perennials: Angelica, oregano, nepeta, foxgloves, hollyhocks, viper's-bugloss, ornamental thistles (Cirsium, cardoons, echinops, etc.), *Verbena bonariensis*, ajuga, geum, campanula, shasta daisy, fennel, etc.

Annuals: Sunflowers, scabious, cosmos, phacelia, anchusa, borage, cerinthe major, poppy, California poppy.

Bulbs: Alliums, *Nectaroscordum siculum*.

Extend the season early and late

It's relatively easy to fill your garden with nectar and pollen-rich plants from late spring through the summer, and your neighbours are likely to be helping out too, but look to maximise your all-year-round planting with both early and late-season flowers for the early and late bees. With climate change, bees are often waking up in winter (at the wrong time of year) and may look for some energy to replace what they've lost.

Early-flowering (winter and early spring)

Bulbs: Snowdrops, crocus, grape hyacinth, winter aconite.

Perennials: Primroses, pulmonaria (lungwort), erysimum (wallflower), asters.

Shrubs and climbers: Daphnes, sarcococca (Christmas box), winter viburnums, mahonia, clematis, ivy, winter honeysuckle.

Late summer and autumn flowering

Trees: Arbutus.

Perennials: Helenium, rudbeckia, agastache, Japanese anemones, bugbane, sedum, salvias and dahlias.

Shrubs: Elaeagnus, *Fatsia japonica*.

Annuals: Dahlias and many annuals will keep going till the first frosts.

plant a nectar bar

A nectar bar sounds fancy but is simply a border packed full of nectar-rich plants with a long season. It's a bit like a pub for insects. If you place some shallow water nearby, they can have a drink, something to eat and no doubt a good chat!

- Choose a sheltered, sunny spot.

- Place each plant in groups or drifts so that the colour and scent are easy to detect.

- Select plants so that you have a good show of flowers from early spring to late autumn.

- Include some night-scented flowers for moths (such as evening primrose, phlox or sweet rocket).

- Always add a few herbs into the mix as they are highly attractive to insects and you can pick some and join in the feast.

Habitats

So, we know that pollinators are all kinds of different insects and the best way to get them to stay once they've had their five-course lunch is to create the right and varied range of habitats for them. I'll look at some, such as beetles and butterflies, within their own chapters, but for now let's stick to bees.

Ground-nesting or mining bees' habitats

We think of bees living in hives but perhaps surprisingly, most species, as we know, are solitary and nest in the ground. Some are the earliest to emerge in spring and many are common in our gardens. The female digs a hole in the ground and builds her nest by herself. You may have seen bees nests in your garden (they look like mini volcanoes). They are usually found in loam and light sandy soils, sometimes pure sand but rarely in clay as it's too heavy going. Now, I usually advocate filling every square inch of your garden with plants but mining bees like bare, undisturbed patches of soil and earth and if you see bees mining in the ground, let them do their thing. Some (three species in the UK) will nest in old snail shells, sealing themselves in with chewed leaves and grass. Clever, eh?

Aerial and cavity nesting bees

These are the ones that will nest in any bee house we make as well as old bird boxes, beetle holes, hollow plant stems or any nook or cranny they find suitable. We can help by making and maintaining bee houses and leaving wooden stacks for them to nest in and overwinter.

making a bee hotel

You will need:

● A plank of untreated wood, at least 10 cm wide.

● A saw, drill and nails.

● Cardboard bee tubes (buy online – recommended as they're easy to use, inexpensive, stay dry and easily changed yearly) or reeds, bamboo canes and hollow stems in a range of diameters.

How to:

1 Cut plank of wood into 5 lengths of 25 cm.

2 Drill guide holes and screw together with the back panel extended as in illustration.

3 Next, using a saw or secateurs cut your tubes, stems, reeds and canes (or a selection of all). Cut to a length of around 23 cm so that when pushed to the back of the frame they sit back about 2 cm which protects them from the wind and rain.

4 Load the frame with your tubes, canes etc. packing them in as tightly as possible.

5 Fix it by screwing it onto a fence or wall. Position it facing south, in a sunny, sheltered spot.

6 This design can easily be adapted to be fixed on a free-standing post in a planting area.

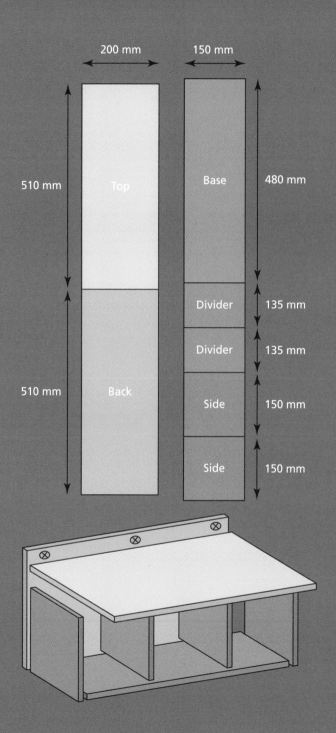

200 mm

150 mm

510 mm — Top

Base — 480 mm

510 mm — Back

Divider — 135 mm

Divider — 135 mm

Side — 150 mm

Side — 150 mm

Maintaining a bee house

Many bee houses are sold, installed and left, or made at home. Some are certainly better than others, so research and shop around. Without wanting to put anyone off doing their thing, it is important to maintain a bee house properly as there is increasing evidence that just by leaving it in place it can encourage parasites, diseases and predators. Some experts say this can have a negative effect on populations. They also only attract a small number of species, so creating long-term nesting sites (such as sandy soil in a sunny spot) is ideal. There are different levels of care, but these are the basics:

- They need to always be dry, as getting them wet can encourage fungal diseases.

- Ideally, have a mix of holes between 2 and 12 mm (some bees are very fussy!).

- They need to be well made, ideally from wood, as soft materials can easily be broken down by predators (tits, woodpeckers, etc.)

- Take them down in the autumn and place in a shed or somewhere dry and cool, and then place back out in spring.

- If you have made one from bamboo canes or gathered plant stems, replace every two years to keep any parasites to a minimum.

butterflies
and moths

I know we shouldn't have favourites but is there a more uplifting sight than gorgeous butterflies fluttering around the garden and landing on something you've planted specifically to entice them in? Moths (divided generally into macro and micro by size) are really just a type of butterfly, being part of the order lepidoptera. Some are just as showy and beautiful as butterflies. Most fly at night – some fly by day too – but if you look closely, the way to tell is that butterflies have clubbed antenna and moths do not. Many other species (birds, mammals, amphibians) predate and rely on them in their various stages (often as caterpillars), so they are an extremely important link in the food chain.

Butterflies (59 species) and moths (around 2,500 UK species) are in huge trouble and I've noticed an enormous decrease of them within my lifetime. My childhood memories of a range of butterflies animating the garden may never be seen again but we must do everything we can to save them.

Decline

A 2015 (*The State of the UK's Butterflies*) report shockingly found that 70% of butterfly species have been declining and 57% 'declining in abundance' since 1976. Moths are in trouble too, with around two-thirds of species in decline and a third of populations dropping by more than 50% over a 40-year period. The decline is down to a combination of factors, including loss of habitat (urbanisation, modern farming methods and increased farmland, loss of hedgerows, etc.). Climate change has led to mild winters and wetter summers. Light pollution, an increase in paved areas and use of insecticides and pesticides are other factors too.

Life cycle

The butterfly's life cycle, called 'metamorphosis', is pretty complicated. They're all different but here's a basic timeline. They start as an egg, which takes around 5 to 10 days to hatch into a caterpillar. In the next 2 to 4 weeks, the caterpillar grows and then becomes a pupa (also known as a chrysalis). The pupal stage can last from 10 to 15 days, and then the adult butterfly emerges. Each of their life stages lasts a different amount of time depending on which species, but on average they have a life span of about two weeks in their adult stage; a painted lady's complete cycle is one of the longest at around 12 months.

Most breed in spring or summer and overwinter as a caterpillar although some get through the winter as an egg, pupa or adult butterfly – told you they were complicated and all unique! The thing is, at each stage they're vulnerable so it's not only nectar-rich plants we need to grow but also we need to provide habitats and perhaps change our gardening methods a little to accommodate them.

Butterflies

Meadow brown

Light-brown with distinctive eyespots on the wings
(complete with white pupils) from June to September.
Commonly seen in gardens, sometimes large groups
flying together. The caterpillars love long meadow
grasses (for feeding and habitats) and the butterflies are
seen on many wild and garden flowers. Overwinters as a
caterpillar.

Orange-tip

The male has white wings with unmissable orange tips and the female has black wing tips on the tops. The undersides are altogether different: spotted green and white and clearly visible when resting. Seen early from April to July. Butterflies visit early-flowering plants like perennial wallflowers (Erysimum), cuckoo flower (*Cardamine pratensis*) and cow parsley. Garlic mustard is great food for the caterpillars. Overwinters as a chrysalis.

Common blue

he male has gorgeous pale blue wings with white fringes; the female has brown and orange wings with a blue dusting near the body. Caterpillars feed on leguminous plants such as bird's-foot trefoil and white clover and butterflies love daisies, knapweeds and other nectar-rich plants. Hibernates as a caterpillar.

Red admiral

Large butterfly with velvety black and white wings with distinctive orange bands. Most migrate back to central Europe for winter but some overwinter here as adults, especially in the south of England. Seen between March and November. Nettles are the caterpillar's main food source and as an adult they'll visit a host of nectar-rich garden plants.

Small tortoiseshell

Gorgeous. Brown body with orange and black wings including white markings and a dark border around the outside. Caterpillars feed on stinging nettles and small nettles, so an essential to the nature garden and adults go for a wide range of garden plants including buddleja and daisies. Overwinters as an adult.

Moths

Cinnabar

Super stylish black moth with tomato red markings on its wings. Spotted from May to August and flies both day and night, so often seen in the garden. They feast on ragwort, which is toxic (so can be dangerous to livestock but very important to around 40 species of insects) so no doubt taste awful, which keeps predators at bay! Overwinters as a cocoon.

Garden tiger

Unmistakeable moth with brown and white wings and an
orange-red face. Seen in high summer around July and
August. The caterpillars are hairy and move pretty fast.
Caterpillars go for a wide variety of garden plants and the
leaves of wildflowers. Overwinters as a caterpillar.

Habitats for butterflies

The best thing to do is to be a little messy or at least leave a part of the garden unkempt. Let some grass grow long and grow a patch of nettles in a sunny spot, which will provide food for caterpillars and a spot to lay their eggs (particularly the comma, small tortoiseshell, peacock and red admiral). A few species hibernate so ideally have somewhere that can be left undisturbed between October and March, perhaps a wood pile or leaves that will also be a good spot for beneficial insects such as ladybirds and lacewings to overwinter in too.

plants for butterflies
(see pollinators too)

Spring nectar: aubretia, bluebell, clover, cuckoo flower, daisy, dandelion, forget-me-not, honesty, pansy, primrose, sweet rocket and wallflower.

Summer/autumn: buddleja, French marigold, ice plant, ivy, knapweed, lavender, marjoram, Michaelmas daisy, mint, red valerian, scabious and thyme.

If you're looking to turn your garden into a wildlife haven, my advice is to make it a fully organic garden. You may have gardened a certain way for years and occasionally used pesticides, weedkillers and chemical feeds but now's the time to move on, look to the future and nurture your outside space for the good of the planet.

No peat

Peat makes a particularly good seed and growing medium for many plants and that's precisely the problem! Around three million cubic metres are used in the UK every year. It's not so much your garden that is affected but the combined environmental cost is enormous and there's no logic in making your outside space a beneficial haven at the expense of another. Peat bogs store huge amounts of carbon and water (so reduce flooding) and make wonderful wetland habitats for birds, butterflies and dragonflies. There are many fine nurseries out there who now grow all their plants successfully without using peat. Ensure the plants you buy in pots and any compost are certified 'peat free'. Peat-free composts contain mixtures of organic materials such as composted bark, coir (coconut fibre), wood fibre and green compost mixed with inorganic materials such as grit, sharp sand and perlite.

No pesticides

Pest control in a wildlife-friendly garden is controversial in itself and some would argue has no place in an attempt to 'play God' and control the natural world. Pesticides may kill the pests, but they tend to be indiscriminate and kill the good guys too. A little like weeds, pests only become a problem if there's an infestation that's upsetting the balance, which will rarely occur in a healthy balanced garden. The fabulous spirit of 'rewilding' in essence lets nature sort everything out itself over time and is a wonderful movement, but our gardens are different in many respects, as they are far smaller and may need some managing and intervention at times (see the organic pest control chapter).

make compost

A compost heap is the engine room of the garden and in some form or other is an essential item in a nature garden. Waste (such as kitchen waste, leaves, prunings, paper, cardboard, etc.) goes in and compost for the garden (to use as a soil conditioner, mulch, in pots and containers or sieved for seed sowing) comes out. Brilliant! Compost heaps, however, are also living things in themselves, full of bacteria, fungi and yeast, which are beneficial and go back into the garden too. A compost heap also attracts all manner of wildlife that live on the decaying material, such as worms and millipedes, and in turn the wildlife that come and feed on them. Frogs and toads may overwinter in them (I would, they're nice and warm!) and hedgehogs and slow worms may nest in them year-round, so be careful when turning them. Bumblebees may nest in them too, so if spotted leave them till the end of summer when they'll die out. Ideally, have two compost heaps, as it makes better compost moving material from one to another and means if one has become a home and is out of action, there's always the second! The more open your compost heap is on the sides, the better it is for access so use slatted wood (or old pallets).

Soil conditioning and mulching

Soil conditioning is all part and parcel of gardening. You may want to dig organic material (your own compost, leaf mould, mushroom compost, well-rotted manure, etc.) in initially, but by mulching in autumn (deeply, around 5 cm). It suppresses annual weeds, and the worms will do the hard work and take down the organic material for you to make your soil more fertile and moisture retentive. Mulching also increases worm and invertebrate activity beneath.

weeds and weeding

You may have heard the maxim 'one year's seeding means seven years' weeding'? And, of course, many would argue, especially in a wildlife-friendly garden, that a weed is simply a plant in the wrong place. Many of them are beneficial (e.g., a patch of nettles for egg-laying moths and butterflies and overwintering insects, buttercups for pollinators). We do, however, need to manage the space and it's the plants that become invasive, get out of control, and smother others that we need to concentrate on. In spring, they grow at a rapid rate if you don't keep on top of them. If you've recently dug over a new patch, you're likely to have stirred up masses of weed seeds that have been waiting for you to come along to release them!

Know your weeds

Some fabulous garden plants naturally self-seed, but when weeding you may be taking them out by mistake. Identifying young weeds means you can get them before they seed so try and get to know the main ones in your garden.

Annual weeds like bittercress, chickweed, herb-Robert and cleavers (sticky willy) flower, seed and die off in one year. The seed dropped is triggered next year. Regularly hoeing them and then picking or raking them off a flower bed will keep on top of them – if you stop them seeding, they'll die out altogether eventually.

Perennial weeds: These are the ones like dock, creeping thistle, couch grass, ground elder, nettles and couch grass. They'll die back in winter and come back every year from the roots and often spread through their roots systems as well as seeding around for a double whammy!

The most pernicious ones: Some weeds such as bindweed, mare's tail and the dreaded Japanese knotweed are particularly difficult to remove. Be patient, keep weakening them and over a few years it can be done.

organic weed control

By hand: Hand pull or hand weed with a fork or a weed knife (with a hooked end). Cut repeatedly to weaken them. With most perennial weeds, if you leave a tiny bit of root in, they'll back so be rigorous.

Flame gun: These are pretty popular for gravel areas, paths, and initial weeding of areas as a powerful one will burn weeds right down to the roots.

Cardboard and mulch: Mulching deeply with bark, compost or other organic matter around your ornamental plants will smother the weeds. Placing a layer of cardboard too, wetting it and then mulching on top with compost

and planting small plants directly into the mulch can work well too.

organic
pest control

So-called 'garden pests and diseases' are often seen as going hand-in-hand with our garden plants. Greenfly, blackfly, slugs, snails, whitefly, vine weevils, etc. are some of the most common critters and rust and blackspot are common plant diseases. They are dreaded by many 'conventional gardeners', some who sadly reach for the chemicals the minute they see one for a short-term cure over prevention approach. I've seen people who stand a foot away from a plant covered in greenfly and spray the hell out of it when they could simply wipe them off in a few seconds!

Chemicals simply don't have a place in a nature garden – every creature is welcome. The healthiest and most sustainable gardens are based on sound horticulture and contain strong growing healthy plants born out of good gardening techniques (right plant in the right place, a wide range of plants, soil conditioning, feeding, pruning, general garden hygiene, tool cleaning, etc.). Weak, susceptible plants are usually a pest or disease's first port of call as the robust ones can look after themselves.

Natural biological control is all part of the garden's natural and often fragile ecosystem. One species feeds on another and in a healthy garden there will always be just enough food to bring in the good guys, the predators. It may rarely result in a complete extermination of what is seen as a 'garden pest' but shouldn't lead to a damaging problem, as a healthy sustainable balance is achieved. The problem with sprays is that they will often kill off the biological control (the predator) themselves and so the problem exacerbates.

Many wildlife lovers understandably wouldn't dream of killing or even discouraging a single creature in their garden and would let nature take its course. Others who say they garden 'with wildlife in mind' may feel they need to manage that balance from time to time in what is, after all, a manipulated environment. You make the decisions; it's your garden.

Biological control

Ladybirds, hoverflies and wasps (yes, they do have a purpose!) prey on pests and many can now be bought online. I introduced some ladybird larvae years ago into my garden when my kids were younger (a great project and the greenfly were becoming a problem then). Ever since we've had plenty of ladybirds and few greenfly, the best £15 ever spent! Predatory mites are used on red spider mite in the greenhouse. Nematodes (microscopic worms) can be used against slugs, vine weevils, leather jackets and chafer grubs in lawns. Mix the solution in water (to the recommended dose, which usually contains around 300,000 of them) and simply water it onto the soil or compost as long as the ground temperatures are above 5°C.

Physical barriers

These are used to avoid infection and infestation and are mainly used in a vegetable garden to protect edibles. Keeping a pest off a plant can be done in many ways and on many scales. The simplest example is a fruit cage to keep birds off fruit altogether, but environmental mesh or fleece will help stop pests getting to them. Cardboard or carpet underlay collars around your brassicas will keep root fly off. Carrot flies are strange things that haven't worked out how to fly over 75 cm high (so how do they fly up a hill?) so growing carrots in tall containers or with a barrier round them usually does the trick.

Pests

Slugs and snails: Look for holes in leaves (especially hostas of course) and slime trails! **Control** – Beer traps (shallow saucers placed at ground level filled with beer, they drown happy), barriers like copper rings, coarse grit and shell mulch. WD-40® sprayed round the top of containers apparently works. Garlic spray on the leaves. Apply nematodes for slugs.

Aphids (sap-sucking insects, including greenfly and blackfly): Look for stunted growth, sticky honeydew and the aphids themselves. **Control** – You can

remove them by hand or with a jet of water, which also kills them. Encourage natural predators such as ladybirds, hoverflies and lacewings (or introduce larvae). Make habitats for the predators such as nooks and crannies or wood with holes drilled in to overwinter.

Lily beetles and rosemary beetles:

Look for holes or chew marks in leaves. The bright red lily beetle (on lilies and fritillaries) and the rather beautiful golden rosemary beetle (on rosemary) are easily seen.

Control – The only real way is to pick off the beetles by hand, start early in spring, and encourage birds to feed on them. Burn spent lily leaves and stems in autumn.

Vine weevils:

Black hard insects that damage leaves and their larvae live in the soil and damage roots. Look for irregular serrated leaf edges (adults) and the larvae attack the roots of pot plants, which causes wilting and sometimes kills the plants.

Control – Catch adults at night using a torch (to find them, not to hit them with!) and use nematodes on pots.

Diseases

Rust: A fungal disease that damages leaves and weakens plants. Look for orange or brown spots on bottom side of leaves (on roses and hollyhocks).

Control – Remove and destroy any affected leaves and those that fall on the ground.
If persistent, look to grow rust-resistant varieties.
Same approach with blackspot.

Powdery mildew: A dry weather fungus that attacks already weak plants. Look for white powdery covering on leaves and flowers on plants like acanthus, hydrangeas, phlox, honeysuckle and roses.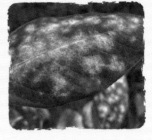
Control – Water regularly and mulch plants heavily to keep moisture at the roots. Cut back any weeds nearby that could harbour the fungus.

Bud blast: A fungal disease on rhododendrons and azaleas spread by leafhoppers. Look for dry brown flower buds with tiny black bristles on them.
Control – Be vigilant, try and remove and destroy any infected buds wherever possible.

Nutrient deficiency: Okay, so this common one is not a disease but is often seen as one and out comes the (useless) spray! Plants that lack nutrients available to them suffer in different ways. Look for leaves yellowing between
veins (magnesium deficiency – use Epsom salts) and curling leaves with brown edges (calcium deficiency – add lime or calcified seaweed to reduce acidity, which makes nutrients more available). Generally, add organic matter to soil to increase moisture retention and reduce leaching of nutrients to keep all plants healthy.

Natural wildflower meadows studded with cornflowers, corncockles, ox-eye daisies and poppies are a summer sight to relish, proving that nature, when left to its own devices, always does it best. Sadly, our UK wildflower meadows have been in retreat because of intensive farming methods and population growth. In fact, we have lost a staggering 97% of them. As well as being beautiful, wildflowers are the lifeblood of many pollinating insects and I'm sure you'll agree, way more interesting than large areas of continually mowed lawn that dominate many of our gardens. Large plots perhaps lend themselves to more naturalistic planting, an enticing path or two mowed through long grass and wildflowers but even in a small space there's always room to grow a few wildflowers in a raised bed or pot.

Annual or perennial

Sowing annual seed is an extremely economical way
to cover a patch of otherwise unused poor soil for one
season (perhaps for a bare patch or an area you've got
future plans for). Annual wildflowers such as cornflower,
tickseed, bishop's flower, corncockle and poppies grow
well on both fertile and poorer garden soils. Seed mixes
don't contain grasses, so butterflies and moths won't
breed in them, but the flowers are long-lasting so
provide a long season of pollen and nectar.

Perennial meadow flowers include plants like
meadow crane's-bill, field scabious, greater knapweed,
yarrow, agrimony, buttercup and ox-eye daisies. They are
slower to establish from seed and require poor soils, but
once they get going, will come back year on year.

Annuals and perennials can be mixed giving you
both a short-term hit and a longer-term wildflower
power plan too. Many perennial mixes include a
percentage of grasses that look great, but these should
only be sown onto poor soils or they'll thrive and
smother the wildflowers over time.

The quick-fix annual summer meadow

Easy annuals can be sown direct on any weed-free patch in plenty of sun in spring and will start to flower around 12 weeks later. Hardy annuals prefer to be sown in autumn to establish themselves but can be sown in spring too (they will then start to flower a little later).

corncockle

cornflower

corn marigold

corn marigold

corn poppy

californian poppies

Dig over, weed and rake the soil and sow directly as the packet instructs and don't be tempted to over sow. You could mix 2 x times annuals to 1 x perennials for a display this year while the perennials develop. Think about mixing your own seed selection or there are plenty of seed companies selling ready-mixed packets too, with a pretty picture on the packet to aim for. The classic flowers are corncockle (pink), cornflower (intense blue), corn chamomile (white daisies), corn marigold (yellow daisy), corn poppy (red) and Californian poppies, but many others such as red orache, *ammi majus* and tickseed are just as easy.

converting a lawn to a perennial meadow

Most garden soils, even under lawn areas, are too rich for many perennial wildflowers and, as a result, grasses and stubborn weeds will romp away and tend to muscle them out of the way. With time and patience, however, the fertility can be reduced, and they too can be developed into perennial wildflower meadows. There are different approaches and which one you choose will boil down to the overall size of the area, your timescale and your gardening oomph (muscle), but as with all gardening, patience is the key to success.

The midterm

Strip the turf by hand or perhaps machinery, depending on its size. Dig out any perennial weeds' roots. Dig over or rotavate the soil and rake to a reasonable tilth. On heavy soils, you can add sharp sand or cover the entire area with sand (sown directly into) but never add organic matter. If you're serious, then you could strip the topsoil off altogether (perhaps with a digger and use elsewhere?)

and rotavate the subsoil beneath, which will be low in nutrients and ideal to sow directly into. Perennial seed can be bought ready mixed or mix your own and sow to the recommended rate (don't be tempted to over sow). Wildflower turf is also available but considerably more expensive (perhaps for small areas?) but always looks great in its very first season.

The slow burner

Stop feeding (and weed killing if you do) and watering the lawn but keep mowing it weekly throughout the year, making sure to remove all grass clippings. This will help weaken the grass a little. Some wildflowers will establish themselves naturally if left unmowed next year. Patches of soil can then be removed and seeded, or plants can be sown and grown in pots and then planted into the lawn for a higher success rate. You can also buy plug plants online or from a garden centre, which will work out more expensive depending on the area size but can be planted into the gaps. Plant in groups of the same plant for a natural look. With all establishing meadows, weed out any invasive plants at an early stage.

The wild card

Yellow rattle (*Rhinanthus minor*) is the wildflower's best friend where grass is dominant. It's a semi-parasitic annual that lives on the roots of grasses and can weaken its hold considerably over two or three years. Cut the grass in autumn, scrape back some large patches of grass to expose soil and sow, letting it self-seed all over before cutting back the following late summer.

maintaining a new perennial meadow

With new perennial meadows, it is important to mow the meadow in the first year after sowing to help thicken it up and develop strong roots. It may still be looking really good (so rather painful to do – no pain, no gain), but cut or mow it to a height of 5 cm after about eight weeks of growth and it'll bounce back and flower again.

ongoing care

At the end of August/beginning of September, cut the meadow area and leave the cuttings on the ground for a week or so and ideally turn them over once or twice with a rake so that the dry seed heads drop all their seed. Then remove all the arisings (cut vegetation) from the area and compost. The idea is not to put any nutrients back into the soil, just keep taking away to turn back time to when these areas were naturally grazed.

collecting
seeds from your
own garden

Most of us buy seed in spring ready to sow but if you look around your own garden from late summer onwards, you'll find it's stocking quite a lot of nature's free bounty. Growing plants from seed rather than buying them ready grown in pots is extremely rewarding. The next level up is one of the most satisfying of all gardening processes: growing plants from seed you've collected yourself from your own or other people's gardens.

Some plants have simple seed heads while others have more elaborate seed storage and drying units, many of which are a picture in themselves such as the translucent papery ellipses of honesty seed or the hard seed cases of poppies complete with shower-proof caps on. So, which to collect? Well, a little experimentation may be required. The seed of species plants will come 'true' (therefore, be the same as the mother plant) but those collected from a hybrid are likely to be extremely variable with each one coming up slightly different. Some plants are extremely promiscuous with every seedling coming up a little different and, who knows, you may produce a fabulous gardenworthy new plant just waiting to be named (the famous poppy 'Patty's plum' was found as a chance seedling growing on a compost heap).

The seed and fruits of many plants can easily be harvested and sown straight away (some actually prefer autumn sowing when fresh), whereas most can be dried and stored for sowing in spring. There's plenty out there. Annuals such as orlaya, cosmos, nigella, zinnias, perennials like verbascums, astrantia, eryngiums, hollyhocks and, for those who grow edibles, there are many vegetables like beans, peas and carrots.

Timing is key when collecting seed. Too early and the seeds won't have developed fully and may not be viable or store well, leave them too long though and they'll drop on the ground in a bid to germinate themselves. Keep an eye out as you move around the garden looking for ripe heads and pods that have dried nicely, brown in colour but are yet to split open. You'll quickly get your eye in and spot those that are ready for harvesting or those that may need another few dry days.

How to harvest seed

What you need: secateurs, paper bag, pencil.

- On a dry day, place a paper bag over the top of the seed heads (singly or with the stalks) and then snip them off. You may want to secure with a rubber band first before cutting. This will stop the seeds shaking off while cutting.

- Label the bag with what plant it is and the date (of harvest). Do this as soon as you harvest each plant before you end up with lots of confusing paper bags!

- Lay the seeds out to dry on a warm windowsill or in an airing cupboard for a few days. This makes it easier to separate the seed from the pods or capsules. If they don't open naturally, help by gently breaking them open to release the seed.

- After extracting the seed, clean off any chaff attached. This is important as it can harbour a host of diseases if left on.

- Once fully dried, put the seed in labelled paper bags, place in an airtight container and ideally put in the fridge (or a dark, cool, dry place) until they're ready to sow.

For fleshy fruits, berries and rosehips, you can also save the seed (often dispersed in nature by birds). It's a different process as the seed heads don't need to be dried, just picked when fully ripe. Collect the hips/berries then squash them in a fine kitchen sieve. Wash away the remaining pulp in cold water till you have the seed. Spread them out on kitchen roll for a few days until

they're dried out and easy to handle. Hardy fruit and shrubs will need stratifying by placing on or between wet kitchen roll or similar and placed in a fridge for a few weeks to mimic a cold winter to make them germinate properly after.

Some annuals to collect and store for spring sowing

Calendula, cornflowers, foxgloves, honesty, morning glory, nasturtium, nigella (sow direct straight after collection), ammi majus (sow direct straight after collection), poppies, Californian poppy, sunflowers and sweet peas.

Perennials to collect and store for immediate or spring sowing

Agapanthus, alliums, aquilegia, delphiniums, hollyhocks, grasses, sea holly.

native hedges

Over recent years, sales of wooden fences have rocketed as owners search for instant privacy and rarely contemplate the slower approach of planting a hedge and waiting for it to mature. I'd love to see more native hedges planted in towns and cities and especially on new-build sites, making them an integral part of the planning requirements. Why not, when double glazing and parking spaces are? Some of the fabulous privet hedges on the Bourneville estate in Birmingham were planted well over 100 years ago and are still going strong.

Hedges and hedgerows tick plenty of the boxes of sustainability and biodiversity. Native hedges provide the perfect natural resource and nesting opportunity for all sorts of wildlife (insects, birds, hedgehogs, voles, etc.) and, when mature, tend to be more effective in filtering and reducing strong winds than hard structures and they help soak up pollution too. They look good too, greening our countryside, towns and cities and reflect the seasons perfectly: flowering in spring, often displaying bright berries and fruit for the birds and many put on an autumnal extravaganza too.

Before the invention of the plastic pot, everyone planted plants 'in season'. They'd see plants in flower in the field, order them and then in the dormant season (Nov–March) they'd be dug up bare-rooted and posted ready for immediate planting. On the whole, bare-rooted plants are way cheaper than pot-grown and often outgrow them in the long run. Deciduous hedges are best planted this way.

A mixed hedge is the best approach for wildlife as it harbours the widest range of invertebrates, which in turn encourages plenty of feeding mammal and bird species. Of course, a mixed hedge may not work with the aesthetics of the garden and if this is the case, limit the range of plants used and simplify it. There are no set rules, but if you want a mixed native hedge then hawthorn (*Crataegus monogyna*) and blackthorn/sloe (*Prunus spinosa*) are the best choices to make up the backbone of around 50%. The other 50% can be a mix of some or all of the following, which all have different qualities for you to choose from.

Acer campestre: field maple with winged seeds and strong yellow foliage colour in autumn; an excellent choice for a large hedge.

Alnus glutinosa: common alder, it has yellow catkins followed by false cones. Particularly good on boggy ground. Another good choice for a large hedge.

Common dogwood: *cornus sanguinea* has rich autumn foliage colour, black berries eaten by birds and green flushed red stems in winter. Medium-sized, can be kept smaller.

Spindle (*Euonymus europaeus*): fabulous autumn colour and cheery rosy-pink and orange fruits.

Dog rose (*Rosa canina*): with pinky-white simple flowers, followed by bright scarlet rose-hips that are loved by small birds for their seeds inside. Medium-sized, can be kept smaller.

Guelder rose (*Viburnum opulus*): has large white flowers followed by bunches of small red fruit and deep-red autumn foliage. Medium-sized.

Other good choices include hazel, crab apple, beech, hornbeam, holly, privet, field rose and briar rose.

How to plant

When you receive bare-root plants by mail order, keep the plants in a cold dark place and don't let the roots dry out. Plant as soon as possible as long as the ground isn't frozen. Plant a double row of bare-rooted whips (rows 50 cm apart) if you have room or, if space is limited, plant a single row or zig-zag them slightly so they have more root room. Spacing depends on which plants you choose but smaller plants should be about 40 cm apart. Prune in the autumn ideally so as not to disturb nesting birds and if you cut quite hard in the first few years, to help them thicken up nicely at the base, they'll repay you over the many years to come.

Trimming hedges for wildlife

In their first year, cut them to around 45–65 cm, which will encourage nice bushy growth. After that, most gardeners tend to clip hedges square and upright, but I say go your own way. I love to see organic shapes and wavy hedges as if they've taken on a life of their own, and it's perhaps an effective way of tying in with a borrowed view if you have one. We're looking to let those that flower and berry do just that (for wildlife) and allow birds to nest in them undisturbed. This means the window to trim them in is late winter or early spring, never in the nesting season (from March to August). If you have a large hedge, consider clipping in sections (and if regenerating an old hedge, cut back in sections) to allow wildlife extra cover and less shock.

rain gardens

Rain gardens are a fine solution within some nature gardens and I've no doubt we'll see more of them in the future designed into new-build homes and retro-installed where possible. You can make your own, the process is pretty simple – a little like making a pond – but do take care when planning in case of them overflowing in extreme weather and make sure you know where any underground services are before digging.

Rain gardens can make up an entire space but tend to be areas within a larger garden that can receive water runoff directed from roofs (such as sheds, extensions, etc. and hard surfaces like paving). Bog gardens are permanently wet whereas rain gardens become waterlogged for short periods and then completely dry out at certain times of the year too so are planted with tough and resilient plants that can cope with those

extremes. They can look great and work well in back gardens, allotments, front gardens and community gardens but not everyone will have the right spot for them. Let the site dictate.

why

Rain gardens are a way of putting the water back directly into the water table rather than directing it down a drainage system. The hard elements in our towns and cities have a huge environmental impact, sometimes causing flash flooding as our drains can't cope with extreme storms and the urban heat island effect shows that cities are significantly warmer than outlying rural areas both day and night as a result of the high percentage of buildings and hard surfaces. Greening them up as much as possible and allowing any water that falls on your footprint to drain back into the ground slowly can only be a good thing.

They can be low maintenance spaces, with opportunities to plant a wide range of perennials, many of which in turn will attract insects and birds to the garden. Once plants have established, no watering should be required. They reduce the effects of erosion too by slowing down heavy rainfall and can soak up around 30% more water than the average lawn. Sometimes, gardens have a soakaway (basically a large hole full of hardcore or drainage material) sunk into an area to cope with heavy rain. A rain garden does the same thing while making a feature of it too.

create a rain garden

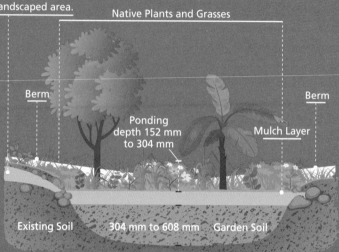

Water can be delivered through a swale lined with plants, a pipe or across a landscaped area.

Native Plants and Grasses

Berm

Ponding depth 152 mm to 304 mm

Mulch Layer

Berm

Existing Soil

304 mm to 608 mm

Garden Soil

How

Rain gardens are best constructed in summer when the ground is dry and then planted in spring for plants to establish themselves. The basic idea is to allow as much of the water that falls on your buildings or garden back into the water table. A shallow dip or sunken area is dug and the water from a roof, or hard surface diverted into it through a rill, pipe, overflowing water butt or rain chain.

Siting

To stop it turning into a pond, it's important to meet some basic requirements.

- Site it in a well-drained area, so the water does drain out of it. Test by digging a decent-sized hole around a metre in diameter and 15 cm deep and filling it up with water and seeing if it drains okay. If it drains slower than 5 cm per hour (e.g., the water level drops less than that rate) it's likely to be heavy clay beneath so unsuitable.

- Site in sun or partial shade for plant selection.

- If placing closer than 5 m to your house, consult a Registered Ground Engineering Professional to avoid any damage to foundations by infiltrating water.

- You can site it where the runoff from a hard surface can be diverted or at the bottom end of a sloping garden, or site it towards the bottom of a natural gentle slope of up to 10% that naturally becomes boggy.

Size and depth

The size will be determined by how much space you have and what surfaces are draining into it.

It should be a minimum of 20% of the roof/surfaces, so say you have 100 m² of roof runoff, the rain garden needs to be at least 20 m² of roof.

Depth depends on how well your soil drains and how much rain there is. They aren't deep like ponds, being between 10 and 20 cm deep.

Making a rain garden

- Remove all vegetation and dig out the shape with a flat, level base and level all around.

- Some of the soil you dig out can be used to make the lip (berm) on three sides, which needs to be well compacted, around 30 cm wide and 10 cm in height.

- Leave a gap in the lip and fill with gravel, so if it completely fills it can flow out. Consider where it'll end up, such as soaking the lawn or going down a drain nearby.

- Dig around 30% extra compost or well-rotted manure into it and in proportion with the spoil and then backfill to its original level.

- Install a downpipe diverter or 'elbow' to the downpipe leading from the roof gutter or make a rill with pipes, bricks or hidden liner with stones placed on to take the rainwater from the elbow to the rain garden.

Planning and planting the rain garden

Place the plants that cope with wetter conditions at the base and add in plants for seasonal interest and those of course that are great for wildlife. Plant in groups (threes, fives or sevens) for impact. Mulch again after planting and every year, and water well for the first year or so until all plants establish themselves.

Good plants for rain gardens
Herbaceous perennials: *Iris pseudacorus, Iris sibirica, Juncus effusus, Zantedeschia aethiopica, Persicarias, Verbena bonariensis,* hardy geraniums, hostas, crocosmia.

Shrubs: *Cornus alba* varieties, *Viburnum opulus*, *Hydrangea arborescens* varieties, *Buddleja davidii* varities.

Grasses: Many *Miscanthus sinensis* varieties, *Calamagrostis brachytricha.*

annuals

If you're planning a wildlife garden over time and planting a relatively empty space or a 'blank canvas' with trees, shrubs, perennials and bulbs, patience will be required. Annual plants provide very quick results as they germinate, grow quickly, flower and set seed in a single season. Regularly deadheading those that produce masses of flowers (not the ones for seed heads to attract birds like teasels and sunflowers though!) tricks them into producing more flowers (and not going to seed). Their flowers and seed are beneficial to wildlife (mainly pollinators and birds) and of course brighten up our gardens too – well, why shouldn't we benefit!

Most are extremely easy to grow and are popped into garden borders, raised beds, containers and hanging baskets after the last potential frost (around mid-May in most areas). They're not only for young gardens so look to plant them out every year. They're not permanent so your colour scheme (crazy and riotous or restrained and tasteful?) can be changed annually – see them as fun and experimental to play around with.

Annual climbers (like black-eyed Susan and sweet peas) are another consideration, ideal for some situations whether you want to add height in a border by pushing a few canes into the soil as a wigwam, for arches and pergolas or to grow up a fence or wall, which they'll cover in a single season.

Sure, you can buy plugs, strips or individually potted plants from garden centres but it's way cheaper and more satisfying growing them from seed, whether you

start them off in pots and plant them out or sow seed direct where you want them when the soil's warmed up. Here's how:

- Soak the seed overnight in jam jars to soften their coating, and if you're sowing more than one variety, make sure to label them!

- Use 10-cm pots filled with seed sowing compost, sow to quantity (some will be one per pot, some more) and depth as the packet instructions.

- They need around 21–24°C (average room temperature) to germinate. Depending on your local weather, you may be able to get them going in a cold frame outdoors (or a greenhouse/conservatory?) or place on a sunny windowsill. If you have an (inexpensive) plastic propagator, then great. Keep the soil nice and moist but not waterlogged.

- Seedlings should appear in 2–3 weeks. Either thin them out to one plant per pot (choose the healthiest) or carefully lift the other plants (hold by the first set of leaves not the stem and use a chopstick to tease them out) and pot on individually.

- Keep them frost free and well-watered. Once they start growing, push a small stick into the pot for the climbers to get them growing upright.

- From the beginning of May, harden off the plants to acclimatise them and toughen them up. A cold frame is ideal for this as the lid can be opened during the day and closed at night or take them out during the day and put inside (but not next to a radiator) at night.

sowing direct

An easy way is to sow directly where you want them to grow. They'll start to flower a little later in the season and you'll have to wait for the soil to warm up a little before you sow. Mid-May is a good time. Prepare the soil well and add in plenty of compost. Plant a few seeds in situ with a view to thinning them out later (possibly move some to another gap?) once they've germinated and grown a little.

Biennials (such as honesty and teasels) are sown one year and flower the next but well worth getting a succession going for wildlife.

For butterflies and bees

Marigolds (*Tagetes*): Spicy orange flowers that don't stop coming all summer.

Stocks (*Matthiola*): Wonderfully scented cottage garden plants that bring pollinators in from miles around.

Honesty *(Lunaria annua)*: Purple or white open and accessible flowers and lovely papery translucent seed heads.

Phacelia tanacetifolia: Bee magnet alert! Hairy annual with finely cut leaves and very dense, curved spikes of small, soft lavender, bell-shaped flowers.

Cornflowers (*Centaurea cyanus*): Prolific in shades of blue and easy to grow and many varieties. Choose native ones if you can.

Cosmos (*Cosmos bipinnatus*): Classy plant for containers and borders in a wide range of colours.

White laceflower (*Orlaya grandiflora*): White umbels of white flowers with tiny sails at the end of the petals. Great for hoverflies.

Tobacco plant (Nicotiana): Strong evening perfume so great for moths. Elegant forms in whites, pinks, purples and greens.

For birds

Teasels (*Dipsacus*): Finches adore pecking seed from the tall seed heads.

Sunflowers *(Helianthus)***:** Such fun plants, some reaching 3 metres or more! Leave the flower heads on for the birds in autumn.

Nigella: Self-seeds around prolifically and the small black seed provides valuable food.

planting a tree

Trees can be bought in containers all year round, but they can also be purchased during the dormant period (November to March, the ideal time to plant) as bare-rooted or root-balled plants. Bare-rooted trees are literally trees that have been lifted out of the ground roots and all, most or all of the soil falls off and they work out better value than container-grown plants, and often perform better in the long run too. Root-balled trees tend to be for larger specimens that have been lifted with their soil kept in situ around the roots with hessian sacking or the like. Both root-balled and bare-rooted trees will have had quite a few roots cut off in this process but don't be alarmed.

when to plant

The dormant period between late November and late February is ideal as most trees will have stopped growing completely and can settle in through the winter and develop roots underground before putting on top growth next spring. Remember: a tree is for life not just for next spring! Do some research about its height, shape and habit and wildlife benefits. I always look for trees that will perform a minimum of twice a year. Deciduous trees such as crab apples and sorbus (ornamental ash) will provide spring flowers, fruit and have a wonderful autumn colour too. That's good value in my book.

When it comes to planting your new tree, there are a few golden rules. There are many approaches and changing theories, but this is how I do it. If you have a wait between delivery and planting, never let them dry out.

- Dig a hole to just below the depth of the tree (use a stick to measure). Be generous with it widthways and break up the bottom of the pit with a fork if the soil is compacted. Mix plenty of organic matter with the spoil. With container-grown trees, dig a square hole to break the cycle of the roots going around in circles.

- Insert a stake into the ground first so you don't cut through any roots later. Drive it at a 45-degree angle low down with the top end pointing towards the prevailing wind. This means the roots will stay solid but the tree can bend in the wind and build up its own innate strength.

- Check the tree for broken or crossing branches or broken roots. Prune them off cleanly and make sure it's a nice open shape. Do this before you plant, as you may not be able to reach later!

- Soak the tree well before planting.

- Place the tree in the hole and leave the hessian/sacking in place as it will rot away and the roots will grow through it. Be careful not to damage the bark at any stage as it can lead to serious long-term problems.

- Use a stick placed across the top of the hole horizontally to make sure that the tree will end up at the same level it was originally grown. There will be a visible mark on the bark on bare-rooted trees called a 'nursery line'. Adjust the soil up or dig down as necessary and make sure any roots aren't curled back on themselves.

- Backfill the hole with the mixed soil and shake the tree occasionally to ensure there are no air gaps. Tread the soil in lightly with your boots, adding into the soil till you reach the surrounding ground level.

- Tie the tree to the stake using a tree tie (this must be quite tight but do check every six months as it will need adjusting).

- Water in well and apply a mulch of organic matter without building up against the tree trunk. Water during dry periods.

index

A

acanthus 162
Acer campestre 181
aconite, winter 127
aflatoxin 71
agapanthus 178
agastache 128
agrimony 165
ajuga 126
alder, common 74, 181
algae 28, 34
Allium 126, 178
Alnus glutinosa 74, 181
Amelanchier 74
ammi majus 169, 178
amphibians 99–108
anchusa 126
Andrena (solitary bee) 120–1
anemone, Japanese 128
angelica 125
annuals 195–208
    deadheading 20, 195
    for pollinators 126, 129
    and seed collection 174, 178
    weeds 154
    for wildflower meadows
    165, 166–9
ants 88
aphids 84
    ant farming 88
    black bean 84
    organic control methods
    158–60
    predators 89, 91, 123,
    159–60
Apis mellifera (honeybee)
118–19, 122
apple 125
    see also crab apple

aquatic plants 31, 32, 107
aquilegia 178
Arbutus 129
ash, ornamental (Sorbus) 76,
    211
aster 127
astrantia 174
aubretia 148
aucuba 79
azalea 162

B

bare-root plants 180, 184, 210
bat boxes 113, 114–16
bats 109–16
    brown long-eared 111
    common pipistrelle 111
    Daubenton's 111
    diet 112
    shelter for 112, 113–16
    soprano pipistrelle 111
bean(s) 174
bee hotels 132–4
beech 183
beer traps 160
bees 22, 117–34
    aerial/cavity nesting 132
    bumblebees 118–20, 152
    ground-nesting/mining 131
    habitat 131–4
    honeybees 118–19, 122
    ivy 121
    leaf-cutter 121
    plants for 202–5
    solitary 118, 120–1, 131
beetles 83–92, 85–7, 112, 119
    chafer 85, 159
    false oil 87
    lily 161

rosemary 161
    stag 86
    swollen-thighed 87
    thick-legged flower 87
    violet ground 87
    water 28
Berberis thunbergia 78
berries 74–9, 176, 182
Betula 76
biennials 201
bindweed 155
biodiversity 7, 10, 18, 26, 180
biological pest control 158–9
birch, silver 76
bird boxes 65–7
bird cherry (*Prunus padus*) 75
birds 28, 35–82
    bathing 64
    diseases 46
    feeding 68–73
    and hedge pruning 185–6
    plants for 74–82, 207–8
bird's-foot trefoil 141
bishop's flower 165
bittercress 154
black-eyed Susan 195
blackbird 37
blackfly 84, 158, 160
blackspot 158, 161
blackthorn/sloe 181
blanket weed 34
bluebell 148
bog gardens 188
Bombus (bumblebee) 118–20, 152
borage 126
brooklime 107
buckthorn 79
bud blast 162
Buddleja 143, 148
    B. davidii 194
Bufo bufo (toad) 102, 107, 152

bug hotels 21, 91
bugbane 128
bugs 83–92
bulbs 20, 126, 127
bumblebee (*Bombus*) 118–20, 152
buttercup 165
butterflies 119, 135–43, 150, 153, 165
    comma 146
    common blue 141
    decline 136
    habitat 146
    life cycle 138
    meadow brown 139
    orange-tip 140
    painted lady 138
    peacock 146
    plants for 148, 202–5
    red admiral 142, 146
    small tortoiseshell 143, 146

C

Calamagrostis brachytricha 194
calcium deficiency 162
calendula 178
callicarpa 79
campanula 126
Cardamine pratensis (cuckoo flower) 140, 148
cardboard 156, 159
cardoons 126
carrot 174
carrot fly 159
caterpillars 136, 139–43, 145–6
Centaurea cyanus (cornflower) 164–6, 169, 178, 204
Cerinthe major 126
chaffinch 49
cherry 125
    bird 75
chickweed 154

Christmas box (sarcococca) 20, 128
chrysalis 136, 140
Cirsium 125–6
cleavers 154
clematis 80, 125, 128
climate change 118, 127, 136
climbers 13
    annual 195
    for birds 79–80
    for pollinators 125, 128
clover 148
    white 141
cockchafer (may bug) 85
compost heaps 96, 108, 112, 151–2
corn chamomile 169
corn marigold 166, 167, 169
corn poppy 167, 169
corncockle 164–6, 169
cornflower (Centaurea cyanus) 164–6, 169, 178, 204
Cornus
    C. alba 194
    C. sanguinea 182
Corylus avellana (hazel) 76, 183
Cosmos bipinnatus 126, 174, 204
Cotoneaster 77, 125
cow parsley 140
crab apple 75, 125, 183, 211
Crataegus monogyna (hawthorn) 75, 125, 181
crocosmia 193
crocus 127
cuckoo flower (Cardamine pratensis) 140, 148

D

dahlia 128, 129
daisy 20, 141, 143, 148
    Michaelmas 14, 82
ox-eye 164, 165
shasta 126
Daisy grubber - A hand held narrow two pronged for like tool ideal for levering out deep roots.
damselflies 28, 88
dandelion 148
Daphne 20, 128
deadheading 20, 195
delphinium 178
Dib - A loose term used when sowing seed or planting small plants or bulbs into the ground with a 'dibber' (a pointed wooden stick).
Dipsacus (teasel) 81, 201, 207
diseases 46, 158, 161–2
dock 154
dogs 95
dogwood, common (Cornus sanguinea) 182
dove, collared 36, 62
drainage 11, 191
dunnock (hedge sparrow) 57

E

early-flowering plants 127–8
earthworm 90, 151, 153
earwig 89
echinops 126
echolocation 110, 111, 112
edibles 118–19, 159, 174
elder 77
eleagnus 129
endangered wildlife 94
erosion 189
eryngium 174
Erysimum (wallflower) 127, 140, 148
Euonymus europaeus 182
evening primrose 80

F

farming methods 118
fat/suet 68, 69, 72
Fatsia japonica 79, 129
feeding plants 150
fences 96
fennel 126
finches 45, 46, 68, 207
firethorn (*Pyracantha*) 78
fish 34, 107
flame guns 156
flash flooding 189
flowering seasons, extension
   127–9
forget-me-not 148
foxglove 125, 178
frogbit 32, 33
frogs 28, 31, 34, 100, 107–8,
   151–2
frogspawn 34, 100,
   107
fruit cages 159
fungal diseases 161–2

G

garlic mustard 140
geranium, hardy 193
geum 126
goldfinch 45, 68
grass clippings 170,
   172
grasses 21, 178, 194
   couch 154
   see also lawns
grasshopper, field 89
greenfinch 46
greenfly 84, 158, 159, 160
ground elder 154
guelder rose (*Viburnum
   opulus*) 78, 183

H

habitats
   for bats 112
   linking together 24–6
   loss/fragmentation 94, 118,
      136
   for pollinators 131–4
hawthorn (*Crataegus
   monogyna*) 75, 125, 181
hazel (*Corylus avellana*) 76, 183
heavenly bamboo 78
Hedera (ivy) 14, 128
H. helix 79
hedgehogs 90, 93–8, 100, 152
   diet 94
   houses 97–8
   safe environments for 95
   and wildlife corridors 24–6
hedge sparrow (dunnock) 57
hedges 12, 179–86
   how to plant 184
   plants to use 181–3
   pruning 185–6
helenium 128
Helianthus (sunflower) 81, 126,
   178, 208
Hemiptera 84
herb-robert 154
hibernation 86, 94, 96, 100,
   102, 106, 141, 146
holly (*Ilex*) 75, 125, 183
hollyhock 125, 161, 174, 178
honesty (*Lunaria annua*) 82,
   148, 178, 201, 203
honeybee (*Apis mellifera*)
   118–19, 122
honeydew 88, 160
honeysuckle (*Lonicera*) 79, 125,
   162
   winter 128
hornbeam 183
hornwort 32

hosta 193
hoverflies 84, 119, 123, 159–60, 205
hyacinth, grape 127
Hydrangea 162
   H. aborescens 194

I

iceplant 148
Ilex (holly) 75, 125, 183
insects 83–92, 112
   pollinating 117–34
   see also specific insects
Iris
   I. pseudacorus 193
   I. sibirica 193
   yellow flag 32, 33
ivy 14, 128
   English (*Hedera helix*) 79

J

Japanese anemone 128
Japanese barberry 78
Japanese knotweed 155
jasmine 125
jay 60
Juncus effusus 193

K

knapweed 14, 141
   greater 80, 165

L

lacewing 112, 146, 160
ladybird 84, 86, 146, 159–60
Lasioglossum (solitary bee) 120–1
late flowering plants 128–9
lavender 14, 125
lawns 22, 96
   converting to perennial meadows 169–70
layered planting schemes 18

layout 9–16
leafhopper 84, 162
leather jacket 159
lemon balm 81
lepidoptera 136
lilac 125
log stacks 16, 91, 108, 112, 146
Lonicera (honeysuckle) 125, 128, 162
L. periclymenum 79
Lunaria annua (honesty) 82, 148, 178, 201, 203

M

magnesium deficiency 162
magpie 60
mahonia 77, 128
maple, field 181
mare's tail 155
marginal plants 32, 107
marigold (*Tagetes*) 202
   French 148
marjoram 14
marsh marigold 32
Matthiola 202
Mattock - A hand tool used for digging and chopping. It has a long handle and a double sided head, one side similar to a pickaxe and on the other a flatter sharp hoe like tool (also known as an adze).
meadow crane's-bill 165
mealworms 72
Mentha aquatica 107
metamorphosis 138
mildew, powdery 162
mint 14
   water 107
Miscanthus sinensis 194
mites, predatory 159
morning glory 178

moths 112, 119, 130, 135–6,
    144–5, 153, 165
    cinnabar 144
    decline 136
    garden tiger 145
mulches 152–3, 156, 215
Myosotis scorpioides 107

N

Nandina domestica 'firepower'
78
nasturtium 178
nectar 124
nectar bars 130
Nectaroscordum siculum 126
nematodes 159, 160, 161
neonicotinoids 118
nepeta 125
nettle 142–3, 146, 153–4
newts 28, 107–8
    great crested 105–6
    palmate 105
    smooth (common) 104
Nicotiana 205
Nigella 174, 178, 208
nursery lines 215
nutrient deficiency 162
nyjer seed 68, 71

O

orache, red 169
oregano 125
organic gardening 149–62
Orlaya 174
    O. grandiflora 205
Oudolf, Piet 21

P

pansy 148
paths 11
paving 11
peanuts 68, 69, 70, 71

pea(s) 174
    sweet pea 178, 195
peat 150
perennials
    for birds 80–2
    cutting back 21
    for pollinators 125–6, 127,
    128
    for rain gardens 189, 193
    and seed collection 174, 178
    weeds 154–6, 169
    for wildflower meadows
    165, 169, 171
Persicaria 193
pesticides 91, 96, 118, 136,
    150–1
pests 7, 84, 157–62
Phacelia 126
    P. tanacetifolia 203
phlox 130, 162
physical barriers 159, 160
pigeon, wood 36, 63
plant supports 212, 215
plug plants 170
pollen 124
pollination 118–19
pollinators 117–34, 153
pond plants 31, 32, 107
pond skaters 28, 84
ponds 14, 27–34
    and amphibians 107–8
    and bats 112
    depth 30
    edges 30
    filling 34
    and hedgehogs 95
    lining 30
    and micro-organisms 34
    siting 28
    using chemicals in 34
poppy 126, 164–5, 174, 178
    Californian 126, 167, 169, 178

corn 167, 169
'Patty's plum' 174
Potager - A potager is
a vegetable garden
that is also designed
and ornamental so is
productive but looks great
too.
predators 7, 89, 91, 123,
159–60
primrose 127, 130, 148
privet 183
pruning 20, 185–6
Prunus
    P. padus 75
    P. spinosa 181
pulmonaria (lungwort) 127
Pyracantha 78

R

ragwort 144
rain gardens 187–94
rewilding 151
Rhinanthus minor 170
rhododendron 162
roads 95
robin 53
rocket, sweet 130, 148
rook worms 85
Rosa 77, 125, 161, 162
    briar 183
    deadheading 20
    field 183
    R. canina (dog rose) 183
rosehips 20, 176
rowan (*Sorbus*) 76
Royal Horticultural Society
    (RHS) 124
Royal Society for the
    Protection of Birds (RSPB)
    36
rudbeckia 128
runoff 11, 188, 191

rust 158, 161

S

salvia 128
Sambucus nigra 77
sarcococca (Christmas box)
    20, 128
scabious 14, 126
    devil's-bit 80
    field 80, 165
sea holly 178
seasons of interest 19–20, 127
seating 14–15
Sedum 20, 128
seeds
    collection 173–8
    sowing 165, 197–201
shade 18, 28, 32
shield bug 84
shrubs
    for birds 77–9
    for pollinators 125, 128, 129
    for rain gardens 194
silver birch 76
skimmia 79
slug pellets 96
slugs and snails 100, 158,
    159–60
snowdrop 127
snowy mespilus (*Amelanchier*)
    74
soakaways 189
soil 152–3, 169–70
sorbus (ornamental ash) 76,
    211
sparrow 65–7, 84
    house 36, 50
spiders 90
spindle 182
Spit - A spit is a
    measurement of depth
    of soil measured by the
    length of a spades head.

One spit is one spade deep, tow is two!
stakes 212, 215
starling 36, 63
stocks 202
sunflower (*Helianthus*) 81, 126, 178, 208
sunflower seed 68, 70
surfaces 11
    free-draining 11
sweet pea 178, 195

T

Tagetes (marigold) 148, 202
Taxus baccata 76
teasel (*Dipsacus*) 81, 201, 207
thistle
    creeping 154
    globe 82
    ornamental 125–6
thrush, song 36, 54
thyme 14
tickseed 165, 169
tits 65–7, 84
    blue 38
    coal 36, 41
    great 42
toad (*Bufo bufo*) 102, 107, 152
tobacco plant (*Nicotiana*) 205
trees
    for birds 74–6
    buying 210
    deciduous 28, 211
    planting 209–16
    for pollinators 125, 129
trichomonosis 46
turf, wildflower 170

V

valerian, red 14
van Sweden, James 21
verbascum 174
Verbena bonariensis 126, 193

Veronica beccabunga 107
Viburnum 20, 128
    V. opulus (guelder rose) 78, 183, 194
vine weevil 158, 159, 161
viper's bugloss 125
Virginia creeper 13

W

wagtail, pied 62
wallflower 127, 148
    perennial 140
wasps 119, 159
water features 14, 26, 27–34, 64, 95
water forget-me-not 107
water mint (*Mentha aquatica*) 107
waterviolet 32, 33
weeding 153–6
weedkillers 150
weeds 153–6, 169
white laceflower 205
whitefly 158
wildflower meadows 22, 163–72
wildlife corridors 15–16, 23–6, 28, 96
winter aconite 127
woodpecker
    green 60
    spotted 60
wren 58

Y

yarrow 81, 165
yellow rattle 170
yew 76

Z

Zantedeschia aethiopica 193
zinnia 174